HACKIE

CAB DRIVING AND LIFE

BY JERNIGAN PONTIAC

These are revised versions of stories first published in the newspapers,
The Vermont Times and *Seven Days*.

ISBN 0-9753056-0-3
First Printing May 2004

Thanks to Donald Eggert and Seven Days Design for cover design and typesetting.
Thanks to *Seven Days* for the newspaper's support in production and marketing.
Thanks to Sarah Ryan for the Hackie illustration.

For additional copies of this book contact the official *Hackie* website:
www.YoHackie.com

Printed in the U.S.A. by
Morris Publishing
3212 East Highway 30
Kearney, NE 68847
1-800-650-7888

Dedicated to the soulful people of
Burlington, Vermont —
the "Queen City," my hometown

ACKNOWLEDGEMENTS

Thanks to Ruth Solomon, Moreno Robbins, Eric Perkins, Erik Esckilsen, Shay Totten, Paula Routly, Pamela Polston, and especially Don Sander.

And for their love and special support, thanks to my two moms, Mrs. Jane Johnson and Mrs. Doris Robbins.

Contents

Foreword BY ERIK ESCKILSEN

Taxi drivers must hear more unsolicited stories than people in any other occupation, except maybe bartenders. I take that back. I've done a little work in both fields, and it seems to me that taxi drivers actually hear more stories over the course of a shift. Besides, owing to the effects of alcohol, bartenders get many of the same stories over and over again.

So, in a way, taxi drivers are part of the storytelling tradition, whether they like it or not. When I was driving the taxi line at Burlington International Airport with Jernigan Pontiac, hearing stories was my favorite part of the job — well, that and having some cash in hand at the end of my shift. Thanks to Jernigan's writing, and our semi-regular breakfasts at a local café, I'm still privy to the kinds of stories that made cabdriving so memorable. Now, with this collection, you can be, too.

But, truth be told, I was a short-timer as a taxi driver. Jernigan is in it for the long haul. He's a real "hackie," a pro, not someone driving a cab until something better comes along. This may not be obvious to his passengers, since Jernigan really drives no better or worse than anyone else. No offense to him. The breadth of his experience, though, is obvious to anyone who has read his "Hackie" column, which was first published in *Vermont Times* and now appears in *Seven Days*, the alternative newsweekly in Burlington, Vermont. Every couple of weeks, Jernigan reminds us that a lot can happen between pickup and destination, even when the ride's just across town.

The other thing that resonates in his writing is Jernigan's full *presence* in his work. How else could he mine the deeper truths in every story he hears, evoke the deeper impulses that compel us humans to reveal ourselves to a complete stranger?

It's tempting to propose that the relative anonymity, and the transience of the cab ride, inspire passengers to be more candid in their disclosures to the driver. But some of the stories in this collection come from Jernigan's regular fares, people he's been driving for years. If they're honest with him, it's not because they think they'll never see him again. They know they will — next time they need a lift. No, it's probably for the same reason anyone ever reveals anything to another person: trust.

As these essays reflect, even the passengers who cross paths with Jernigan only once leave behind their own tales of the human experience like so many gum wrappers tossed on the floor. Tales of yearning. Of failure. Of a desire to be safe, to connect, to just *be*. What lies at the heart of Jernigan's stories is the heart itself.

This collection does what no other book has ever done: It captures the essence of a hackie's work. I used to think being a cabdriver meant simply getting people from one place to another. Reading Jernigan's stories, I realize it means helping people find their way home.

My Blood Runs Yellow

When business is slow, I find myself reflecting on a quarter-century of hacking — that is, cabdriving. I think about a twisting, turning, pot-holed road that somehow stretches from my native Brooklyn, New York, to the roads I now love best, here in gentle Burlington, Vermont. My thoughts often come around to this question: Are taxi drivers born or made? And if business is *really* slow, I go back to the very beginning of my journey. And I mean the very, very beginning.

As a youngster, my toys of choice were trucks, trains and racing cars. I had my first two-wheeled bicycle by age six. In seventh grade, I delivered the *Daily News* every morning before school. I counted the days till I got my driver's license at age16. And all through my childhood, I was fascinat-ed by taxis. Cruising the city streets, picking up all kinds of people, learn-ing about life and making money — hacking has had a hold on me for as long as I can remember.

On the day of my eighteenth birthday, I headed for downtown Manhattan, to the Taxi & Limousine Commission, and took the examina-tion for a New York City Hack License. The exam ostensibly tested the applicant's knowledge of about a dozen important City locations such as the Empire State Building, the Port Authority, La Guardia Airport and the like.

It was the early seventies — a decade before the deluge of Asian and African immigrants who now comprise the bulk of New York cabbies — and the taxi fleet owners were hurting for drivers. Wanted: sentient human being willing to drive cab. Total ignorance of the New York City street grid was not, in their view, a significant hindrance. I guess the owners applied pressure to the Commission, because, in the hallway outside of the testing room, there were stacks of "study sheets" which provided the answer to each exam question. As if this was insufficient prompting, the proctor didn't stop you from bringing these cheat sheets with you into the exam. Under these rigorous conditions, I think even the desperate fleet owners would agree that anyone failing was indeed too stupid to drive.

The next day, freshly minted license in hand, I presented myself at a large taxi garage near Borough Hall in Brooklyn. I had long black hair tied back in a ponytail, and a scruffy beard. I wore seldom-washed old dungarees to go with my oversized, mottled green army jacket. I presented my license to the owner and was hired on the spot. Off-and-on for the next four years, I would drive cab for the Ken-Bright Taxi Company.

My first day on the job, reporting for the night shift, there was no company orientation. I mean none whatsoever. I entered a large waiting room for my vehicle assignment. This is known as the "shape-up"and was choreographed with dictatorial aplomb by a scary looking guy with a pencil-thin mustache. Jerry sat on a high stool, ensconced in a caged-in booth situated about three feet above the floor level of us peons. It was not unlike the physical lay-out of the set of the late-seventies television show, *Taxi.* The chief difference between that show and my actual experience was the dispatchers. On *Taxi,* the Danny DeVito dispatcher character, Louie, was far more gentle and compassionate than real-life Jerry.

After about a half-hour wait, I finally heard, like a bark from a perturbed rottweiler, "Pontiac — what kinda fuckin' name is that?" I waved my hand and he tossed me down a set of keys, along with a helpful instruction — "Make some money."

Out on the lot, I found cab #22, a fairly new, beautiful Yellow Checker. It was, and still is, an urban tank — shaped like a bloated brick with two circular fold-up seats located in front of the rear bench seat. Between the front and rear was a pathetically flimsy Plexiglass "shield" mandated, I later discovered, by the union contract. I took one look and decided, if a customer pulls a gun, I will give him my money in a New York minute.

I climbed into the driver's seat and it felt wonderful. The taximeter sat perched on the dashboard to my right, a clunky metal box with a foot-long arm and handle. (This was a decade before the advent of computerized digital meters.) I had taken the occasional taxi ride as a civilian, but how exactly did you work the meter?

Luckily, at that moment, the grizzled day driver appeared, thermos in hand, at my door. He asked if I saw his Pall Malls. They were there on the dash, and I handed them over. I told him it was my first day and inquired of him how to work the meter. He showed me. I then reached for the seat belt but couldn't find it. As he turned and walked away, I called out, "Hey, where the heck are the seat belts?" Without breaking stride, he replied over his shoulder, "Don't worry about the belts. We cut 'em out — they just get in the way. Good luck, kid."

I fired up the Checker and headed north on Flatbush Avenue towards the Manhattan Bridge. Before I reached the bridge, a tiny, ancient black lady hailed me. I pulled over, she climbed in and told me her destination, just a few blocks up. As I pulled up to her apartment building, I told her it was my first day on the job, and she was my first customer. She smiled warmly and said, "Good for you, young man." She handed me the fare, which was less than a dollar, and a quarter tip. God, it felt great!

Twenty-five years later, dropping someone off at Nectar's Restaurant on Main Street in Burlington, Vermont, it still feels great.

My life's journey has been anything but a straight road. The one constant has been hacking. I keep coming back to it. Taxi driving has been my therapy, my Zen retreat, my finishing school. It's where I've learned who I am — perhaps the hard way. Behind the wheel, I've also met untold amazing people. Well, untold until now . . . .

Jernigan Pontiac
Spring 2004

1

Regulars

There are customers who are my "regulars". In some cases, I've been driving them for years. Some of them are boisterous and unguarded; others intensely private. But either way, I have a connection with them; I'm part, however small, of the fabric of their lives, and they of mine. And, through the years, I learn their stories.

George

George is in his mid-fifties. He's short, maybe 5'5", and pear-shaped, like a large gumdrop. When you look closer though, you notice his arms and hands are powerfully muscled. He's balding with wide gray eyes covered by thick lens glasses set in old-fashioned black frames. The glasses don't quite fit, so he periodically adjusts them with a nudge of a thick finger.

George has taken my taxi scores of times, a few trips a month for years, anyway. I like him a lot. The two of us are great talkers, and that's why I know a fair amount about his life.

Southern Vermont is one big blur to me, so I forget the name of the town, but George grew up and has lived his entire life in one of the major ski towns in the southern part of the state. Since reaching adulthood, he has held but one job: dishwasher at a large, well known restaurant that caters to the hungry tourists. He lives directly across the road from the restaurant in a cottage owned by his employers. I believe the apartment is provided to him rent-free, or perhaps he pays a nominal charge.

He is an incredibly diligent, and I've got to believe, productive work-er. His work week entails any number of hours, but he's usually given a couple of days off, generally Monday and Tuesday. He has a few weeks off when the place closes during mud season, and also between the foliage and ski seasons. During those breaks, he draws unemployment. On his regular days off, he often takes the Vermont Transit bus from his hometown, trav-eling north to Burlington. When he gets off the bus, I'm usually there.

This is what George does in Burlington. Month in and month out, his routine is a marvel of consistency.

His greeting is enthusiastic, almost gleeful, as if my presence at the bus terminal is a rare serendipity. He says, "Hey buddy, how've ya been? It's been a while."

I load his single, worn suitcase into the rear seat, and he sits in the front next to me.

"I need to go to the Best Western," he says, "but, if it's okay with you, I'd like to first stop at the package store". When I reply, "Sure George, no problem", he says, "Oh man, you're so good to me", and gives me an affectionate squeeze on my shoulder. That never fails to give me a warm fuzzy. I'm utterly serious. The guy's way of being is so genuine, so entirely lacking in guile, that merely being in his presence is a delightful experience.

He comes out of the liquor store, and I wait while he carefully slips the bottle into his suitcase and gets back in his seat for the ride to the hotel. He loves the Best Western. One time, at my suggestion of a "change of pace", he stayed at the Comfort Inn. He proclaimed it "okay", but said he missed the regular place, and that was the end of that radical experiment. Once in the taxi, he tells me his plans for the evening, as if I didn't already know.

"I think when I get to my room I'll put on WJOY — you know, the 'easy listening' station — take a shower, and have a few pops. Could you pick me up at six o'clock and take me down to Crabber's?"

George has a personal lingua franca, which I've slowly absorbed through the years. 'Crabber's' I recognize as George-speak for the popular local restaurant, 'Carbur's'.

"Later on," he says, "I'll go to Perry's for the little neck clams. Oh man, they have great clams there!"

Before we reach the hotel, he invariably removes a five dollar bill from his silver money clip, folds it in quarters and almost furtively passes it to me. "Put that in your pocket", he says in a bass whisper. "That's for you." He then pays me the actual fare when I drop him off.

When I return to the Best Western a little before six, I see he's already waiting at the front desk. He comes bounding out of the lobby wearing a bright blue suit and striped tie. He has a great tie clasp, and his aftershave is of the dark spicy variety. Having downed a few "pops", his bonhomie, which was effusive earlier in the day, is now positively infectious. It takes all of my will-power not to call it a night, and just take in the night festivities with him.

Sometimes I believe that among us walk a few special souls. I like to think of them as the "Bearers of the Fairy Dust". Seemingly devoid of ulterior motive, and always without public notice, these folks go through life with no off-switch on love. They're not saints by any means. They may har-

3

bor deep tragedy, and their personal lives may reveal the occasional ethical shortcoming, but somehow, in their wake, good cheer and joy abound. Without these souls, the world is a sad and arid place, perhaps even uninhabitable.

George, I think, is one of them.

Victory on Main Street

"Take me to the Airport," Ray said. Ray Victory is a local guy — and I reserve that term strictly for "born and bred" — with a toothy smile and a mop of red hair the years have barely muted. As he sat beside me in the taxi, the smile was in high gear. "I'm picking up tickets to visit my cousins in California!"

"California?" I said. "That's great, Ray. But were'ncha out there just a few months ago?"

"Yup, I sure was. But after last weekend, Jernigan, I can't get out of town fast enough."

Ray is a favorite customer of mine, a guy I've driven for years. He smiles a lot, though he's generally griping about one thing or another. The two top targets of his opprobrium are imbecilic politicians, and "the little pukes" — i.e. obnoxious and/or clueless students.

I respect Ray's political opinions, because in contrast to the vast majority of us, he's not just talk and (maybe) the biennial check-in at the voting booth. Ray is a long-time functionary in local Democratic politics, and he genuinely knows a thing or two about what transpires in the body politic. As regards our college students, for a dozen years Ray has managed the downtown Champlain Farms, a regular stop for students on beer, cigarette and junk food runs. If anyone is better-versed in the intricacies of state liquor law, I've not met that person.

Ray has a collection of seized IDs large enough to wallpaper a small kitchen. Like a kid with a collection of Pokémon cards, Ray has gleefully honored me with the show-and-tell. My favorite belongs to one Juanita Gonzalez — a 31 year-old New York City resident, 5'9", black hair. Ray took that particular card off a petite, blonde-haired girl, who, according to Ray, appeared too young for a learner's permit, let alone 21 for purchasing alcohol — let alone 31 and living in Spanish Harlem.

"Mister, you don't understand." Ray mimicked in a surprisingly credible version of a whiny teen-age girl. "That's, like, an *old* picture of me."

The prior Saturday night, a man had walked up to the counter of Ray's store, pointed a gun at him, and said, "Give me the money." Now, a week later, Ray is still shaky. It happened in a flash, without a hitch — Ray said the guy was clearly a professional — but there's no diminishing the psychological aftermath of a gun in your face with ill intent.

Arriving at the airport, I pulled into the service lane and waited while Ray went into the terminal to pick up his tickets. When he returned, and we began the drive back to his house, I knew there was something I wanted to say about the incident.

"Jesus, man. Maybe you should take a session with a shrink. You probably got what they call, 'post—traumatic shock'. I mean, even cops are required to get counseling if they're involved in a shooting." I paused and thought for a moment. "At least that's what happens on 'N.Y.P.D. Blue.'"

Ray tilted his head and raised his eyebrows. "You do know the difference between reality, on the one hand," he said, signaling with both hands to the right, "and television on the other?" He signaled to the left. "I'm just checking, Jernigan. You understand that? Merely checking." He had that crooked grin going again.

"Real funny, Ray," I replied. It actually was pretty humorous, but I was determined to press my point. "Hey — I'm not kidding. That was one hairy experience you've been through."

"Look, I hear what you're saying and I appreciate it," Ray said. He sat quietly for a moment, brushing a hand through his thick hair. "Do you know what the worst part of it was? The deadness in his eyes, Jernigan, the total lack of human emotion. That's the image I can't shake. That's why I'm still so spooked. A cockroach farts in the house, for crying out loud, and I jump."

We pulled up to Ray's place. He got out, stepped to the rear door and removed a large paper bag containing his dinner. From the redolent tang of gravy, turkey and fries it could only be Nectar food.

Ray spoke again through the open rear door. "I gave my notice. It's time to move on. The robbery was just that straw that broke the camel's back."

"Wow, Ray — I'm stunned."

"Yeah, I'll work weekends for a while, until they break in a new person to take my place. I got offered a full-time bookkeeping job with some local bar owners, and I think I'm gonna take it."

I hate when stuff changes, most acutely when it involves the people in my life. I'm almost pathological about it. When I buy my pretzels and Hershey bars, I want to see Ray behind the counter. I want to give him a hard time, to crack the same old, dumb jokes. When I drive him in my taxi, I want to hear new tales of outrage about wayward college students.

I said, "Well, best of luck with it; I'm sure you're making the right move."

That's what I said, but what I felt like saying was, "Ray, what were you thinking? How dare you go out and modify my safe, little universe?"

Angela Gets Old

"How about running me up to The O.P.? There's got to be some fun at one of these places; I just got to find it. You know what I'm saying?"

Angela's stroking her long, honey blonde hair as she sits in the back of my taxi. She's also smoking a cigarette. A few years ago I began to enforce a no-smoking-in-the-taxi rule. As a concession to my regular customers at the time who smoked, however, I let them continue to smoke in the cab under a "grandfather" clause, and Angela's one of those holdovers. One of the advantages in being an independent taxi driver is the Papa Doc Duvalier-like power you wield over the sovereign mini-nation that is your taxi.

In her face, there's lines — around the mouth, across her forehead. She's wearing a lot of make-up, too much blush, but it doesn't appear like she's blushing; what it looks like is camouflage make-up. It's a face that chronicles a long, hard life. If people came with odometers, it would be a quick glance to check the miles. This would be handy, because, as with cars, it's not so much the years as the miles. At times you can look at a person and see the miles. Don't ask me how, but you can see it in the eyes. With certain people, every road traveled is in the eyes. Looking in Angela's sorrowful, clear blue eyes, you can see she's been down some hard roads, though I don't think she's yet reached her mid-thirties.

"Sure, Angela," I say, "maybe something's going on at The Other Place. It's worth checking out anyways."

Flash back 10 years, Angela walking down Church Street on her lunch break, and she could stop a clock. "Walking" doesn't do justice to the sight of Angela, circa 1992 — on her lunch break, maybe it's early summer — prancing, skipping, floating down the promenade, following the gray granite-block centerline. She's wearing a ruffled denim miniskirt, colorful, strapped sandals, and her silky hair cascades down the back of her flowered blouse. There's a movement to her hips, but no hint of trying, no intentional allure — just a natural swing, a young woman fully occupying a beautiful body. She is a vision incarnate of the summer girl: all hope, possibility, and the promise of a bright future.

The past decade has not been kind to Angela. She's been in and out of relationships with a succession of men; nothing seems to last. I remember one guy she went out with in the mid-nineties for what seemed like a couple of years. He was very tall and rangy, with thick, straight hair, and a perfectly groomed goatee and moustache. He was a man with a big, easy smile and a big energy to match. The two of them walking together arm-in-arm or holding hands was a picture of vitality. They were, as people say, a strikingly attractive couple. Maybe it was the demise of this relationship that cut too close to the bone, that dampened her spirit and dulled her inner light.

The truth is, I don't know Angela all that well. Though I drive her often, she stays private, keeps her thoughts and feelings close to the vest. She's always been friendly with me, but not open. That's been fine. I tend to let my customers establish the tone of whatever relationship they have with me. With Angela that tone has always been, and remains, cordial.

"Hey, Angela," I say, "whaddaya think of this frigid weather? Did you see the steam coming off the lake today? It was like it was boiling, not freezing."

She leans forward a little in her seat to respond. "It's crazy all right," she says. "I used to like it more. The chilly Vermont winters — it was, like, invigorating or something. Now, well it's just kind of depressing."

I look up at the rearview mirror, and for a moment, really take in the person sitting back there. It occurs to me how beautiful women become as they age into their thirties and into middle-age and beyond. As I have seen my own youth fade into the distance, I've grown to appreciate the beauty of older women — the wisdom and strength that's earned, and that resonates in their eyes, and bodies, and voice. What's sad, sometimes heartbreakingly so, is a woman trying to freeze age 20 as the years roll on. Sure, I understand — though, as a man, I'll never truly know — the intense societal pressure women face to project youthful beauty. But I disagree vehemently with John Mellencamp who sang, "Hold on to 16 as long as you can." Change is hard, yet holding on is a losing game.

Now my mind is really in gear. I want to say to Angela, let it go — you were once that girl, but let her go. Let yourself be the amazing woman you now can be. And that's me to a tee: Mr. Gratuitous Advice — constantly impelled to enlighten this person or another, as if I've walked in their shoes, as if I've been granted some insider information on how they should live their lives. My God, I can barely manage my own.

You working late tonight, Jernigan?" she asks as we pull up to the bar. "Will you be around to come get me later?"

Jeez, there's still that sparkle in her eyes. "Sure thing, Angela," I answer. "You just call and I'll be there."

Dinner for One

"Hey, Katey," I said, as she entered my cab at a downtown taxi stand last Friday night. "Kinda early to be blowin' town, isn't it?"

"Hello there, Jernigan!" she replied, visibly startled. "I didn't realize it was your taxi when I got in. Gee, I'm sketchy these days."

What a strikingly handsome woman, I thought, not for the first time. She has that dark-eyed Irish twinkle, with short black curls and a lithe, athletic body to match.

"And yeah," she continued, "it is early. But you never feel more alone than when you're alone downtown. I just want to get home to the baby." She shook her head wistfully. "I really don't know why I go out anymore, anyway."

I spun the vehicle around, steering towards Shelburne. Katey lives in an opulent home, next door to her parent's yet more opulent estate. The family — which includes more kids than I've been able to count, though at one time or another, I've driven all the siblings in various configurations — is one in a small group of powerful and wealthy entrepreneurial clans which define the local business and social elite. And like the Pecors, Pomerleaus and Farrells, Katey's family is acutely civic-minded, always looking at ways to leverage their wealth and influence to make Burlington a better place for all of us. This town is blessed, it occurred to me as we drove south on Route 7, with some genuinely decent rich folks.

"How is the baby doing?" I piped up. "She must be getting ready to walk this spring."

"Oh, Erin's toddling around already! The next time he has her, Steve said he's taking her golfing if the course is opened up. I'll give him that — he's really a good father."

Steve and Katey, high-school sweethearts, king and queen of the prom, appeared to have it all. After the five-star wedding, Steve went to work in his in-laws' construction and development business. A few years later, Erin was conceived. While his wife was pregnant, Steve cheated on her — with more than one woman, if I remember the story as Katey told it to me during a ride home last fall.

Propelled by a fierce pride, in short order Katey filed for, and was granted a divorce. The dream she had had for her life was over. All the money in the world does nothing to ameliorate that pain.

"Listen to this, Katey," I said, as we glided past the endless string of hotels and restaurants. "I could see why you don't want to date just yet, and that's probably a good idea for a bunch of reasons. But what about socializing with your friends? Between you and your brothers and sisters, you must know half the young people in town. I mean, you shouldn't be eating dinner out alone on a Friday night."

Katey didn't respond, and glancing over, I could see the pain in her dark eyes. Oh crap, I thought to myself, I'm always inserting my pungent observations into situations where discretion would be the better choice. But like so many cabdrivers the world over, I guess I'm stuck with that fatal personality combo: nosiness and extroversion.

"Hey, I'm sorry," I said, trying to fill up the awkward silence. "That was out of line. I was being kind of pushy right there."

Katey turned toward me, and half-smiled, her eyes filling up. She's one of those people who just can't mask their emotions.

"No, it's quite all right," she spoke softly. "The truth is, since the divorce, my old friends don't want me around their husbands. I mean, it's not like they actually say this, but I can tell. I don't know if they're afraid I'm out to steal their men — and how ludicrous is that? — or maybe, in their eyes, I've become a Typhoid Mary, like I carry the disease that kills marriages. It's like, not only did my marriage fall apart, but I no longer seem to fit in anywhere."

She placed her fingers over her mouth, dropped her head and closed her eyes. I noticed three ornate silver bracelets on her left wrist, and immediately imagined they came from her grandmother, or some ancient Irishwoman even further back in the family tree. Maybe they can work like amulets, I thought, transmitting positive energy, lifting her spirits during this dark stretch of the journey.

After a few turns, we pulled up to the family — well, "compound" I want to call it. The last streaks of sunlight were still dancing over the lake, which was a short walk from their backyard. On the sprawling emerald lawn between the houses, the family was barbecuing. A three-sided tent adorned with colored flags was serving as a kitchen, and what looked like a small kindergarten of little children were running around chasing fire-flies.

As we pulled to a stop, Katey's father approached us, Erin wriggling in his arms. As Katey stepped out of the cab, her daughter jumped down and smothered her with hugs and kisses. If anything is going to carry Katey through the post-divorce emptiness, this is going to be it, I thought.

"I'm glad you came home early," the old man said, and wrapped a still muscular arm around Katey's neck, planting a big kiss on the top of her head.

"Me too, Daddy," she said. "I'm glad I'm home, too."

Friday Night Special

March is all slush and potholes. This one came in like a lion, hung around like a lion, and went out like a lion. The saving grace is spring's inevitability. Hang in there, I exhort myself, as I idle at a downtown taxi stand. Winter *will* die. This tag-on season of frost heaves is merely the death throes.

"Hi there, buddy. Gosh, darn — here I am again. I always get your cab, every Friday night."

The man peering in my window has black, almost grayish eyes, and woolly hair of a similar color. It's hard to tell if it's the approach of middle age; perhaps his hair has always been that hue. He's on the small side, with short arms and rounded shoulders; on first impression, his silhouette evokes the semblance of an oversized gnome.

"You sure do, Carl," I respond. "That's how I know the weekend has begun in earnest, when I drive you home."

"Yup, yup, it's Friday," he says, climbing into the front seat. "Here I am!"

Carl is a guy who will carry on this kind of conversation ad infinitum. *Yes, here you are, and, yes, it's Friday, and I do seem to drive you every Friday.* He's wild about nodding, and agreeing, and reiterating the obvious. When he really gets hold of some riff, it becomes a call-and-response prayer, like we're chanting or something. It's up to me to change the channel, or we'd never move on to another subject.

"The usual, Carl?" I ask. "Headin' home? Stoppin' for a sandwich?"

"That's right! You got it, buddy!" His delight at my recall of his routine knows no bounds. "Yup, I'll be needing a stop at Handy's . Got to pick up a sub for mom."

Carl lives with his mother on Elmwood Avenue. He works in construction, and goes out — apparently by himself, as I've never picked him up or even seen him with a companion — every Friday night. He doesn't exactly close down the town; a few hours at a couple of bars, and he's looking for his cab ride home at 10 or 11.

I gather his mother resents this weekly abandonment, and the sub and beer he brings home is the price of appeasement. This is just a guess though, pure speculation on my part. For all I know, he simply loves his mom, and she loves subs, and there's no subtext.

I pass the Roxy Cinema and take a left into the parking lot of Handy's Downtown Quick Stop. "Do ya need anything, buddy?" he asks, as he steps out. "A soda or something?"

"No, I'm good. Thanks for asking, though."

Glancing through the window of Handy's, I see I'm going to be waiting a while. There's the typical, pre-party Friday night rush of beer, cigarettes and junk food patrons. I don't care how long Carl takes; I'll only charge him one extra dollar for the stop. That's because — gosh, darn! — he's a local, I like him, and it's my taxi company.

About 10 minutes later, he's back in the cab, toting a paper bag. As we pull back onto Winooski Avenue, I notice his right hand is wrapped in a fairly serious-looking bandage.

"My goodness, Carl," I say. "What'd you do to your paw? That looks like more than a paper cut."

"Well, it was pretty dumb. The last time I was at Sh-na-na's, I danced with this girl I liked, and then I saw her outside the club kissing this guy. So I got real wound up, and I went back in the bar and had some more drinks. When I got home, I went in the basement, and I guess I punched a hole in the wall. Yup, I'm pretty stupid, huh?"

"Hey, I don't know about that, man," I reply. "Women can make you crazy, that's for sure, But you don't wanna get self-destructive about it. You know what I'm sayin'?"

"Oh, yeah. Yup, you're right about that." Carl presses his lips tight together, and he's nodding with extra oomph. "My mom was pretty darn angry about the whole thing. She heard the noise and came running down the stairs. She said, 'See how I told ya? This is *exactly* why you shouldn't be goin' downtown.' Maybe she's right, I don't know."

"Jeez, Carl. There's nothing wrong with going out once in while. You just don't wanna get so worked up that you're punching out the walls, that's all."

"Yup, yup," Carl replies, head nodding vigorously again. "Shouldn't get so worked up; I got to remember that."

Slaloming around the potholes, we pass the post office and federal building, and come up on Carl's home. It's a compact, two-story cape, tattered around the edges, modest even by the standards of this aging neighborhood. I come to a stop and click on the four-ways. Carl pays the fare, and gathers up his bundle.

"I got mom her favorite," he says, before closing the door, "ham and cheese with the hot peppers. This'll make her happy." Carl is smiling and nodding. "You know," he adds, "she really looks after me."

"I'll bet she does," I reply. "See ya next week, Carl, and take care of yourself."

"Thanks a lot, buddy," he says. "You're always there for me, every Friday night."

Smiling Buddha

"So what's the problem, Huong? D'ya got a toothache?" I asked my customer as we drove north on Shelburne Road *en route* to a dentist's office at Twin Oaks.

"No, no," he replied. "No cavity — nothing like that. I just get them cleaned. It's for my job. With clean teeth, you get better tip." With that, he chuckled, and offered a wide, exaggerated grin, as if to illustrate the point he was making.

Huong waits tables at the Peking Duck House, in my opinion the finest Chinese restaurant in the area — and I've been a Chinese food fiend since I was a kid. He's been taking my cab for about a year.

"Is that right?" I said, tilting down the rear-view mirror and scanning my not-so-pearly whites. "D'ya think that'd help me? Maybe that's my problem."

"Oh, no!" Huong replied, not missing a beat. "You lousy driver; *that's* your problem."

Huong kills me. His timing is better than Jerry Seinfeld's.

What a life this guy has lived, as American as chitlin's, tacos and knishes. He was born during some of the heaviest fighting of the Vietnam war, or what was called in his country, the American war. It was 1971, in what was then still North Vietnam. I'm still not clear how he pulled it off — and that's probably a story unto itself — but he managed to immigrate to the United States in '96. After a couple of years living and working in the Manhattan restaurant trade, he made it to Burlington just before the century turned.

"Hey, I've been meaning to ask you, how d'ya communicate with the cooks? Some of them only speak Chinese, right? I know this because I often drive those guys."

"No problem," Huong replied. "I speak Chinese. I learn in New York. Two kinds of Chinese I talk. Some cooks from south, some from north. You got to speak both."

"Huong, you are too freakin' much," I said. "You speak about five languages, and I can barely speak English."

"Don't be so impressed," he said. "It's survival. You learn too if you had to."

I contemplated that as we drove along 1-89. The road crews were out picking up and bagging the trash that had accumulated during the winter. Man, I thought, it's great to see the ground again, even if it's still brown. Life in Vermont seems to revolve around the changes in season. How do people live in places where the weather hardly varies throughout the year? And what's it like for Huong, I wondered? What does the Vermont winter feel like to a person who spent most of his life in a tropical jungle climate? Interesting matters, but I had a more pressing question for this customer.

"Talking about tips, Huong, what's the biggest one you ever got? I got a 50 once, myself."

"I beat that," he replied with a laugh. "I tell a customer once that I know the number of every dish on the menu. There's more than a hundred, you know."

"Yeah," I said, "you know how much I eat at the Peking Duck. I love that place."

"So," he continued, "the guy say, 'Is that so? I pick a dish, and if you guess the number, I give you a hundred bucks.' Then he say, 'Spicy eggplant with garlic,' and I say, 'That's number 104,' and he hand me a hundred-dollar bill."

"That's a great story, Huong, and it kinda made me hungry. But, that doesn't qualify as a tip, man. I'm not quite sure what to call it, but it ain't a tip."

Huong laughed and said, "I think you just jealous, Jernigan."

We pulled into the Aesculapius Medical complex, and found Huong's dentist's office — no small task in this prairie-dog village of doctors and dentists.

As he pulled out his wallet, I asked, "How's the Peking duck at the restaurant? That's gotta be their signature dish, I would guess."

Huong stopped counting out the fare, and looked at me intently. "I never eat that duck," he said, "or any other kind of meat. My family is

18

Buddhist for 16 generation. We believe eating meat is violent, and Buddhist is non-violent."

"Wow!" I said. "That's terrific that you're carrying on the family tradition in your new country." We then sat there for a moment, just nodding our heads.

I found myself looking at this guy — this Vietnamese Chinese-food waiter, by way of Manhattan — with new eyes. He's survived war, impoverishment, communism and New York City — all the brutality this dog-eat-dog world can throw at you. And yet, he holds onto to his gentle belief system, and the core value of non-violence.

"So, tell me this," I continued. "How good is the spicy eggplant with garlic?"

Huong grinned broadly, his teeth looking pretty darn clean, even before the treatment. "Number 104," he said, "is very, very delicious!"

2

The Young and
the Reckless

*I drive a taxi in a college town, so many of my customers are students,
and young people in general. And like the rich, the young are different.*

Buffalo Student

For the Great Plains Indian Nations, the fabric of their economy, their culture — their very lives — was interwoven with the buffalo herd. Who could forget the awesome scene in *Dances With Wolves* when, after weeks of searching, the Sioux hunters crest a hill and come upon a veritable ocean of buffalo. In that single ineffable moment, the tribesmen are flooded with a life-giving knowledge: The cycle of life has been renewed. This one magnificent beast provided sustenance to an entire people.

At the height of the summer, I think it was the second week of July, a few of us veteran cabdrivers gathered in an alleyway adjoining the Blarney Stone bar in downtown Burlington. It was just before dawn, no one was about, and that includes, most importantly, the police. We were there to perform a sacred ceremony, and as such, it was not for public consumption. In fact, as far as I know, it has never been limned in written form, only passed down from generation to generation via an oral tradition. I only now commit it to writing having been so instructed by my inner Taxi Spirit Guide.

We use this location next to the Blarney Stone because it is a dive. Not merely a dive, but the Greg Louganis of dives; the one most venerated by the Students — which is the whole point of this secret ritual. By their dedicated presence, they, the Students, have consecrated this site. So, in a very real sense, it is they who have chosen it, not us. All this may seem esoteric to the uninitiated, but to the true Taxi Warrior, it is simply the Revealed Way.

Although most of us have reached middle age, we were dressed that night in the manner of young adults, 20 year-olds to be precise. These were ritual garments we had collected throughout the previous year in anticipation of this yearly gathering. Though these rites date back to antiquity, this is a living, evolving tradition: Each year the clothing changes with the current fashion of the young. Further, in order to achieve maximum spiritual resonance, we mimicked the various sub-genres of the Student population: The frat crowd, the neo-hippies, the St. Michaels Boston townies, the Trinity College goddess worshippers, etc.

We were grateful once again this year for the participation of Mary, one of the few older female cabbies, who that night wore a black, slitted mini-skirt, and a tank top with the bra straps showing — this in evocation of some daring preppie co-ed. Like the rest of us, Mary was too old for the outfit — though I personally thought she looked kind of cool — but she understood the requirements and she's nothing if not a trouper. Prior to her joining the ceremony, the spectacle of one of us grizzled guys dressed up like a sorority girl was not, I assure you, a pretty sight.

We stood in a circle, at the center of which was placed a bottle of Magic Hat beer — a local favorite — and a textbook, this year, *Introduction to Microbiology*. The subject is irrelevant, so long as it is an actual assigned text at one of the local colleges. One of us brought along a small boom-box and cassettes by three local bands: Belizbeha, Strangefolk, and of course, the mighty Phish.

We stood in silence, gathered our concentration, and I popped in one of the cassettes. We then began moving slowly and rhythmically in the circle. After a few minutes of silent movement, the chant began. It arose spontaneously, first barely a whisper, and then grew to a low bass rumble, "Like whatever, whatever, whatever. . . It's all good, it's all good. . . . Like whatever, whatever, whatever. . . It's all good, it's all good."

This circling and intonation continued for approximately a half-hour, although experientially it seemed as if time had frozen. Most critical was the focus of our collective attention: We were calling upon the Great Taxi Spirit to deliver unto us a bountiful Student herd come September. We asked humbly, with feelings of prayerful gratitude, because just as the buffalo was to the Plains Indian, so too is the Student to the Burlington cabbie. And just like these Native Americans also subsisted on fish, berries and various small game, we local cabbies transport the Quebecois tourist, the little old lady, the office and factory worker, etc. But the Students — they are our buffalo, the heart of our economic well-being.

You might ask what's the point of performing the Student Dance? Of course the Students come back every year at this time; it's the beginning of the semester, for crying out loud! To this I can only reply: That's what the

Sioux said about the Buffalo, and look what happened to those guys. We veteran cabbies are not taking any chances.

Now it's the first week of September, about 11 in the evening, and I'm idling at a Main Street taxi stand. I notice a lone young man in baggy pants wandering towards Rasputin's. My heart beats faster — could it be? Then a group of young women are pausing in front of The Last Chance, and then all at once, they're everywhere! Dozens of college kids are streaming down the hill, getting out of cars, and filling up the downtown streets.

Tears begin streaming down my face, and I silently say a prayer of thanks. The Students are back, and all is well in the universe.

Four-Twenty: A Primer

The date was April 19. As I glided into downtown, I noticed the synchronized blinking orange-and-gold marquis lights of the Flynn Theater. Call it "art deco", call it "retro", call it "cheesy" — I dig it. The Flynn — along with Nectar's Restaurant — are as Burlington as you can get. My attitude is, long may they shine.

The Flynn lights are aglow only on show nights, and, as I drove by, I scanned the marquis to see who was playing. The big, black block letters read, "The String Cheese Incident". I had no idea.

Idling at the taxi stand, I absent-mindedly noticed a profusion of latter-day hippies milling about. Colorful, scruffy people were frolicking in City Hall Park, camping on the sidewalks, skipping barefoot along Main Street. We're talking dreadlocks, long patchwork skirts, Birkenstocks, American Spirit cigarettes — the whole nine yards. In this, the hometown of Phish, we're certainly accustomed to the presence of this segment of youth culture. But this night, for some reason unbeknownst to me, Burlington was looking like Woodstock III.

My next fare — a call from a couple of St. Mike's students bound for the concert — cleared up my middle-aged cluelessness. The String Cheese Incident, these students informed me, were one of those rollicking, jamhappy bands so favored by the erstwhile Grateful Dead gang. Hence the downtown hippie hordes.

Sometime pre-midnight, the show let out. Shortly thereafter, I was hailed by a group of the concert-goers, three guys and a young woman. They were high, and I don't mean merely on the good vibes of the Cheese concert they had just attended. Although it's been 20 years for me, you never forget the pungent aroma: These folks reeked of marijuana smoke.

By way of full journalistic disclosure — or is it "disclaimer"? — let me state for the record that, in common with many of my baby-boomer peers,

I "experimented". In my case, the experiment was a resounding success: Unlike some heads of state, I did inhale. Deeply. I passed much of my late teenagedom in a smoky haze. I haven't, however, touched the stuff since the Carter administration, so I'm not exactly up to speed with the customs, favored bands and general modus operandi of your present day stoners.

"Feathers," the young woman said, leaning over the front seat to address her friend, "that was, like, the bomb! It felt like I was at a Dead show."

"No way, Tanya," Feathers replied. Of the four of them, this guy appeared the most entirely stoned. Feathers was slowly listing in his seat as if aboard the deck of a sailboat adrift upon mildly choppy seas. "It sucked. It was just a bunch of hippies dancing. No way you can compare it to a Dead show."

The guy's vehemence struck me as over the top, particularly considering he could barely keep his eyes in focus. I thought, here's a guy who might truly appreciate the Grateful Dead joke.

"Hey, man," I said. "What'd the Deadhead say when he ran out of acid?"

Feathers turned and looked at me like I was from Neptune and speaking Neptunese. From the back one of his friends pitched in: "We dunno. What?"

"Jeez, this music *sucks*," I said.

Laughter exploded from the rear. "Dude," Tanya said, "that's, like, hilarious."

Feathers glared at me in disbelief. "What the hell does that mean?" he said.

"Dude, it's, like, a joke," Tanya said.

"It's not funny," he replied.

"Ya got a better punch line?" I asked, not aggressively, but out of genuine curiosity. What, pray tell, might Feathers come up with? I did not go unrewarded.

"Yeah," he said. "The dude goes, 'What the hell happened to all my acid?'"

Now we were all laughing with raucous abandon, including Feathers. His sheer goofiness was funnier then the joke itself. If there's really such a thing as a "contact high", I think I caught it.

At that moment, the church bells began the twelve tones signifying midnight.

"Woo-hoo!" Tanya said. "It's April 20th — that's four-twenty. Time to party!"

"Okay, that's the second time I heard that today," I said. "What's the deal with 'four-twenty'?"

Feathers began chuckling. "Dude," he said. "Four-twenty is, like, the international time for dope smoking. So, like, 4:20 in the morning is the time to totally toke up."

"Yeah, and on April 20th, that means all day!" Tanya added.

"Well, thank you guys," I said. "You have taught me something I did not know."

I'd like to believe I'm still in the loop, but I haven't been since, say, 1982. It's not as if you're in the loop one day, and out the next. Loop eviction is a slow, drawn-out affair, allowing rich opportunity for self-deception.

But that night — the memorable night of four-twenty — the fog had at long last lifted revealing the glare of naked truth: I am officially and definitively out of the loop.

My God, I think the 12-steppers are on to something: Admitting the truth *is* the first step to healing. I feel better already.

Magic Hat

"Hey, Johnny Q, don't worry about it. There's always next weekend."

The young man sitting beside me was attempting to console one of his two friends in the back. It was a late Saturday night, and the three of them were returning — sans-female being the apparent sticking point for Johnny Q — to the town house they shared at St. Michael's College.

"Don't 'Johnny Q' me," his friend shot back. "I haven't had a date since last spring semester. You're just rubbing it in big-time."

I glanced up at the rear-view and saw Johnny's seatmate give him a shove. He then began to address him in mock-serious deadpan.

"Didja ever consider it might be your personality, Johnny? Because knowing you for three years, I'm telling ya, there's your likely stumbling block."

Johnny smacked his friend on the crown of his head. The force of the blow fell within the realm of "just playing", but not by much. "Screw you, Mikey", he said. "I'm, like, for real here. What *is* my friggin' problem? Wouldja please tell me?"

I turned onto the highway heading north. I always take the interstate to St. Mike's. For reasons unclear to me, I've seen cabbies go via Winooski, but I don't think it's a close call.

I considered the three young men in my taxi, and smiled inwardly. Hacking affords me the opportunity to spend a lot of time with younger folks, and I carry a great fondness for my collegiate customers. I remember, so many . . . sigh . . . moons ago, when I, too, was young and stupid.

They talk so much about sex, particularly the guys. In a nutshell, this is their concern: They really, really, *really* want to have sex.

Mikey relented on the ribbing — maybe the head whack had its desired effect — and said, "Yo, don't ask *me*, man. Why don't you ask the stud, the 'Man-who-Can', our very own Ronster?"

Johnny lightened up, and gave a chuckle. He leaned forward, plain-tively placing his chin atop the front seat. It was a surprisingly touching gesture coming from such a pumped-up, aggressive college guy.

"Ronny," he said earnestly. "Dude. You have hooked up — what? — like every single weekend this semester. And each girl a total honey." Ron looked at him and shrugged, almost apologetically. "School me, Ronny-san," Johnny continued. "Take me under your wing. Be my Obi Wan Kenobi.

I glanced at Ron, and he back at me — sheepishly if I read it correct-ly. I was taken aback by the guy's apparent track record with women. This kid doesn't look the part of some ladies' man, I thought. I mean, he wasn't unpleasant-looking; he just appeared sort of average, your typical healthy, easy-going, 20-year-old. Wherein lies the apparent sexual magnetism? The only unusual aspect of his presentation was the off-white baseball cap, which sported an exceptionally long bill.

"Look," Ron said. "I've been telling you guys all year: I have no frig-gin' idea. I'm the same slacker I was in our freshmen, sophomore and jun-ior years. I, like, can't explain my phenomenal run of luck this year. Like I told you, it must be the hat; that's my only explanation. I've been wearing it every time I hooked up."

Mikey burst out laughing. "Johnny Q, I told you about the hat, did-n't I? We've been rubbing that sucker every night before we go out. It's all in the bill. It's got some special powers. It's strange and awesome, man!"

With that, Mikey reached forward and over Ron's left shoulder, and gave the hat bill a few quick pats, like he was petting a Golden Retriever.

Ron shooed him away, but I could tell he liked the minor legend that had grown around his sexual prowess and good-luck charm. And why shouldn't he? For many people, the college years — the escapades, friend-ships, love affairs — turn out to be the high point of life, the time they felt most free, alive and potent. Bruce Springsteen sings about the "glory days", and my sentiment is, enjoy it while you can.

I pulled the guys up to their living quarters, the "300" town houses. Ron paid the fare, while in the back, Mikey and Johnny Q continued to laugh and goof with each other.

"You know what, boys?" I said, as I folded the money and placed it in my shirt pocket. "If the hat mojo gives you confidence, stick with it. You can give a guy a jelly bean marked 'Viagra', and if he truly believes it, sure enough it'll get him up and at it."

The guys quieted down, their attention momentarily piqued. "Just remember," I added, donning my fatherly hat, "Use the powers wisely. Be respectful and genuine with every woman you're lucky enough to get with."

"Yeah, riiiight!" Mikey said, his sarcasm verging on disdain. Johnny Q, meanwhile, just rolled his eyes. The two of them then got out, and I watched as they walked up to their town house.

"Hey, man, I know what you mean."

I pivoted in my seat to face Ron. In the moment of that discordant exchange with Mikey and Johnny Q, I had forgotten about him.

"Those guys are exaggerating about my success," he said. I wanted to say, "What a surprise," but kept quiet.

"The thing is," he continued. "I *have* hooked up with two women this year, but it's not just fun and games. I really like these girls, and I do appreciate them. A lot. Both of them, in different ways, have taught me something about myself. I don't know if that makes any sense."

I said, "It makes a lot of sense, Ron," and smiled broadly. "You know, I don't think you really need that hat."

"Yeah, you're right," he said, returning the smile. "I guess I'll give it to one of the other guys."

2: THE YOUNG AND THE RECKLESS

A Frosh Perspective

"So what's hot tonight, Jernigan? Where's everybody going? C'mon, give us the word."

A bunch of my freshmen girls were out for another night on the town. Leela sat in the front next to me, and her four compadres were squeezed into the back. Among this circle of friends, Leela was the ringleader, and as such, generally rode shotgun. As usual, the bouquet permeating the taxi was none too subtle; 18 year-old women, I've come to learn, favor sugar-sweet fragrance, and lots of it.

"Well," I said, "tonight I've taken one group to that apartment on Isham, and a few folks to that house on Bilodeau Court. It was rockin' pretty good at the Bilodeau house; that puppy's probably gonna be broken up by the cops earlier rather than later."

Giving out this kind of info, I felt like a weatherman, or better yet, a traffic reporter.

"Downtown's not too busy yet," I continued. "There were no lines at the bars, anyway, when I left to pick you guys up."

"Cool," Leela said. "We're heading to Isham Street tonight. I just broke up with another jerk of a boyfriend, and I'm gonna drink my sorrow away."

Many of my steady customers are students. Of these students, most are freshmen, and of those freshmen, most are women. Upper-classmen are permitted to maintain cars on campus, and even those sophs, juniors and seniors without cars have friends with cars. That's why the freshmen are, by far, more likely to end up as fares.

Why mostly women? When you call a fleet taxi company, you never know which driver they will send. While most fleet drivers are fine, upstanding citizens, a small fraction are what the kids call, "sketchy". Because I'm a solo, independent cabbie, my customers know they always get me when they call, and they feel safe riding with me. My catalog of character defects is legion, but a masher, or flasher, I'm not.

Heading down Main Street, Leela sat downcast, while her seemingly oblivious friends laughed and gossiped in the back. She was an effortlessly beautiful young woman in the flush of youth, with long auburn hair tucked behind her ears, and large, soft brown eyes. Yet she seemed to carry a weight on her heart too great for her years.

The radio was gently playing, and I turned and spoke quietly, something like, "Hey, there's a lotta fish in the sea" — something brilliant and insightful like that. I didn't expect the reaction I got.

"Every single one of my friends has divorced parents," Leela said, with clarity and intensity. "When I was a sophomore in high school, my mother, who's very religious, told me that she didn't love my father at all, and was just staying with him for, 'the good of you and your two brothers.'"

Her eyes glistened with misty tears. "I want to be married one day. But I know that I'll get divorced. Nobody stays together anymore. So, like, what's the point?"

My job is to safely transport people from point A to point B. God knows, I haven't the training nor emotional intelligence to play therapist or counselor. Though I try my best to maintain these clear boundaries with all my customers, I'm least successful when the paternal instinct kicks in. And actually, that's okay with me.

"Listen to me, Leela," I said. There must have been something in my tone of voice, because she turned to face me with unmistakable attentiveness. "Here's where you get to be an adult, to become your own person. I'm sure your mom has many great qualities you want to emulate, but how she's gone about her marriage may not be one of them. You get to do things differently. There's no destiny with this stuff; you know, we're not bound to make the same mistakes as our parents."

"You think so, Jernigan?" she asked.

"Leela, you can take it to the bank," I said with a smile. "And while we're at it, drinking may not be the healthiest way to cope with your sorrow." I gave a chuckle at my own portentousness. "So how heavy is that?"

Leela laughed, for the first time since she got in the cab. We pulled in front of the house on Isham, they all split the fare, and I watched the five of them sashay into the apartment.

Three hours later, Leela called for a ride back to her dorm. There was raucous music in the background, and her voice was slurred.

On the ride over to pick her up, I thought about Leela and her friends, and that portion of the college students who are the binge drinkers. Night after night, semester after semester, I transport them to the clubs, bars, frat parties. What part do I play in this thorny social phenomenon? It's ironic — my economic fortunes tied to these over-indulging students.

Leela wobbled into the taxi. I wondered what had became of her friends. She now looked neither happy nor sad. What she looked was lost. Boy, I thought, my little lecture really helped.

"You know what, Jernigan?" she said. "Life sucks. You know that? Life, like, totally sucks."

"Point A to point B," I whispered to myself. I glanced over at Leela. She was staring blankly into the early-morning, deserted streets. Well, I thought, at least she's getting a safe ride home. And tonight, that's going to have to suffice.

Wheels of Justice

Chatting amiably one evening with a customer as we rolled down the Main Street slope into downtown, I eased to a stop in traffic right at the multi-colored neon sign fronting the Midtown Motel. The intersection of Main and Winooski is less a bottleneck with the recent creation of designated left and right-hand turn lanes. Even so, those of us continuing straight on Main were backed up five or six cars. I'm not a crowder; I respect a proper buffer zone between vehicles. So there I idled, about a half-car length behind the Toyota in front of me.

The green light shone, and the lane began to move. Just as I raised my right foot from the brake pedal, a Jeep Cherokee swung a U-turn from the lane to my right, crossing directly in front of me — inches actually — and I stomped the brake to avoid a collision. "Yow — that was close!" my seat mate erupted.

In the next instant, the Jeep was to my left, facing the opposite direction, inexplicably stopped. I mean, would you linger if you had just executed such a dangerous and reckless maneuver? In shock and anger, I pivoted in my seat to face the renegade vehicle. Despite the chilly late November air, the Jeep's roof was down, and I was confronted by six hot-headed joyriders — probably college fraternity brothers if I had to guess. They glared at me, laughing and jeering.

"What's a matter, cabbie? Something you wanna do?"

Now I understood why they had stopped. It was an opportunity to mock me, to add the insult to the injury. I sat dumbfounded, dumbstruck, and generally, just plain dumb. But what could I have done, anyway? Could I have charged out of the taxi and taught them a lesson? Should I have said: "Boys, that was no random act of spontaneous beauty, senseless kindness, unfathomable camaraderie, incomprehensible conviviality. No, it was downright nasty, and I believe deep down you all know that. Now I want each one of you to step out of that Jeep and apologize to me and my customer." Was that a viable rejoinder?

No, I think not.

I was in the distasteful process of swallowing my anger and slouching on down the road when a miracle occurred. It was a rarefied moment of immediate and transcendental justice. In its perfect timing, it brought to mind the scene in a Woody Allen movie wherein his character gets into an argument with a man in front of him on a theater line. The guy, a perfect popinjay, had been lecturing his date on the subject of Marshall McLuhan. Unable to restrain himself, Allen engages the fellow, challenging his opinion. With a sneer of utter condescension, the man explains to Allen that he is a professor of communications, and, moreover, teaches a graduate seminar specifically on McLuhan, so don't even try.

"Oh, really?" says Allen. "I just happen to have Mr. McLuhan right here." The actual Marshall McLuhan then steps from behind Allen, and tells the man, to his complete mortification, that he, the professor, has totally misinterpreted his theories, and that, basically, he is a moron. Allen then looks into the camera, breaking the fourth wall, and says, "Don't you wish this would happen in real life?"

Well, sometimes it does.

From the parking lot next to Bard's Home Decorating, a siren went off, and the blue lights suddenly filled the streets. The Burlington Police — putting the lie to that musty rhetorical gripe, "Where's a cop when you need one?" — lined up behind the Jeep like a bull moose in rut.

"Pull your vehicle over to the curb."

The sound of a miked officer emanating from a patrol car is like nothing entirely corporeal. Think of the voice of God, or, at least, one of His prophets. To me, in that moment, it sounded mellifluous.

I caught, with thrilling glee, the instant when the faces of the Jeep boys went from self-satisfied smirks to panic-stricken dismay. It was a Kodak moment. I made a mental memo to pick up one of those disposable cameras.

The car behind me beeped, and I got moving. "Did you see that, man? Was that great, or what?" my customer said, with evident relish. "Did I ever!" I replied. "That was a thing of beauty."

I dropped the man at Mona's next to Union Station. My next pick-up was back to UVM. Cresting the hill at St. Paul Street, I could see the blue lights still flashing in front of Bard's. I couldn't wait to revisit the scene of the crime.

Approaching the spot, I saw there were now three police cars in action, and thought, could this possibly get any better? I slowed down to a crawl, and noticed the Jeep driver standing on the sidewalk, an officer at either side, engaged in what I believe is called a sobriety "field test".

I couldn't restrain myself, and why should I have? I stretched over, opened the passenger window wide, and stuck my head through it. "Hey," I yelled to the kid. He turned with a startle. I shot him my broadest, toothy grin.

Pointing to my head, I said, "Remember me? Remember me?"

The utterly woebegone expression on the young man's face took me aback. Slowly, he nodded once, and I believe I detected genuine remorse. It was almost enough to make me feel some sympathy for him . . . but not quite.

Driving With Intent

The two big guys stepped from the door of What Ales You, and slumped into the rear of my taxi. With the demise of the Blarney Stone and the legendary Chickenbone — along with the dislocation of The Last Chance as a byproduct of the Flynn Theater expansion — What Ales You has emerged as the bar of choice for the St. Michael's cognoscenti. It was still early in the evening, but these guys had clearly had their fill, and then some.

"Hey, Mr. Cabbie," one of them spoke up, draped unnecessarily over the front seat. "Couldja take us to the 200 townhouses at St. Mike's? Ya know how to get here?"

"I think so," I responded. "The first 30 to 40 thousand times I took somebody there, it was a little confusing, but I think I got it down now." I hate it when I get sarcastic, but sometimes it just flies out of me. I guess I was bushed, and in a crappy mood to boot. Luckily, these guys were so soused they couldn't distinguish sarcasm from orgasm.

"Right on," the guy replied. "And couldja change that radio station? How about 'IZN or the Buzz?"

"All right — let's try IZN, 'cause I can't cope with the Buzz."

Just then it hit me. Don't ask me how I knew, I just did. Call it a "sixth sense" — except I don't see dead people, I see deadbeats. All of a sudden it washed over me: these dudes were planning to bolt. Maybe it was their conspiratorial whispering in the back; maybe it was their demeanor or attitude. As I said, don't ask.

Right at that moment during the ride, I should have asked them — casually, off-handedly, not wanting to show my hand — to pay the fare in advance. But I didn't, because when push comes to shove, I still doubt my hunches, and I didn't want to insult them.

Thank heavens fare jumping is the most heinous crime committed against us local cabdrivers. In the big cities, cabdrivers are subject to armed robbery, assault and worse. Here in Burlington, the worst that happens is — maybe once every few weeks — a fare runs from the cab without paying. It's infuriating nonetheless, and we harbor murderous feelings toward the perpetrators. Of course, we don't act on these intentions, because that would be wrong, not to mention felonious. Except, as it turns out in this case, I kind of did.

We arrived at the college, and I pulled into the wide handicapped space marking the entranceway to the sidewalk which webs throughout the 200 complex. One guy got out on the right, and began walking onto the path. The other exited on the left, and stepped over to my window. In a play you know, if you have the script, what's coming next. And that's just how I felt. It was eerie.

I lowered my window, and said, "That'll be eight bucks." He took out his wallet, and even went so far as to flip it open and fuss with the billfold. Then he incongruously slapped the top of my cab, and took off in the direction of his now running friend. It was not at all sudden — due to his drunken state — nor was I even slightly surprised. As I said, I knew the script.

In that moment, however, I went off script. I was supposed to plaintively watch them scatter into the housing complex, cursing them, first out loud, then under my breath for the next half-hour as the night dragged on. Instead, I improvised.

I gunned the accelerator and shot onto the sidewalk, steering right at them. I have no explanation for this action, short of momentary insanity — a defense, it's said, the jury never buys. The truth be told, under the right — or wrong — circumstances, I've been known to veer towards reckless impulsive. This was such a circumstance.

Because the sides of the path were piled high with plowed snow, they could only flee forward, and I maintained a steady pace exactly five feet behind their heels. It was like the running of the bulls at Pamplona, me being a bull, and they a pair of unwitting runners.

The headlights — now switched to high beams — illuminated their backs as they clamored ahead. They kept glancing over their shoulders, their eyes saucer-wide in disbelief. They slipped, tumbled, arose and still I came. Through my windshield, they appeared thoroughly freaked out, the picture of abject panic. *If this cabbie is crazy enough to drive on a sidewalk, he could just as well be sufficiently insane to run us down.* I knew this was running through their minds, and I loved it.

One of them finally hurled himself over the snow bank to his left, and escaped. The other managed to scurry around to a series of doors on the ground level of one of the apartment blocks. I came to a stop facing him, the headlights trained on him like an escaping convict. For added effect, I began flashing the high beams on and off. He scrambled from door to door, feverishly searching for an unlocked one. The last door was the charm, and he disappeared into the townhouse.

At that point, I could have called St. Michael's Security and had him busted. But I didn't want to waste anymore time, and besides which, I don't think they countenance sidewalk-driving, even under these exigent circumstances.

More importantly, I no longer needed the money, nor craved justice. I had already gotten eight dollars worth of satisfaction.

3

Tough Customers

My skin is thick. Twenty years of cabdriving has that effect.
My tolerance for boorish behavior is exceedingly wide, but it's not infinite.
Every so often, a fare can be — let's say — challenging.

Joanie

It's a quiet, late Tuesday night in downtown Burlington. The students are in their dorms — Tuesday is not one of their big nights for bar-hopping. Weekends — beginning with Thursday night — you can bank on a lot of student runs. The other four nights are touch-and-go. Twenty-plus years in the taxi business and I've yet to discover how they seem to collectively make this decision, and don't think I haven't given it a lot of thought.

The baffling, if not cosmic, aspect of the nightly migration down the hill, is its all-or-nothing quality. Like wildebeest on the Serenghetti plain, you rarely spot just one or two. It's the whole herd or nothing. How does the word get out? Is it posted on the Internet, or does an inner Gen-X clock instinctively move them downtown *en masse*? I am — as those very students would say — clueless.

Without the students, nightlife activity is at a minimum this bracing, early spring evening. I'm parked at a downtown taxi stand turning the ignition on and off, and, with it, the heater. I hate wasting gas but it's cold. I'm seriously weighing packing it in when a grizzled regular appears at my window.

"Take Joanie home for me, will ya?" he says.

Standing, wobbling next to him is a disheveled friend, a drinking buddy for the night is my guess. The woman has seen better days. That's no problem for me. Take away the intoxicated clientele and the taxi industry — worldwide, I imagine — goes belly up. Working the night shift you learn to be around drunkenness or you quit the profession.

My regular helps his friend into the back seat and heads back to the gin mill. I give her my usual, "Where we going?", look up at the rear-view mirror and await the answer. It doesn't come.

I turn in my seat and look at my fare: Frazzled, smeared make-up, could be 40, could be 65. A lifetime of hard living has a way of eroding the accustomed facial aging indicators. Again I prompt, "Anywhere in particular?"

Her pale blue eyes lock on me, and she whispers, "Take me home."

I reply, "Gladly, but you gotta give me an address."

Now understand, I want to take her home. It's my mission — I take folks out, and I take folks home. I garner both money and a sense of purpose from doing this. I watch this woman in the back seat try, really try, to recall where she lives, but the alcohol has taken her beyond this cognitive awareness.

It's a slow night; I give her a good five minutes to come up with this crucial piece of information. When it becomes clear it isn't going to happen, I ask her to please leave the cab. Her blue eyes shine at me like two, small stage lights, and she repeats, like a prayer, "Please, take me home."

I put the car in gear, ease out of my spot and drive up parallel to a parked police cruiser a block away. I flick on the four-ways, roll down the front passenger window and give the officer the run-down.

The officer knows my customer by name, but not, unfortunately, where she lives. The cop asks her nicely, but she's not going to leave the taxi. "Joanie," he says, "we can do this the easy way or the hard way, it's up to you."

Joanie has staked out a position tonight, and that position is no retreat, no surrender. She's staring at the officer, but says not a word.

For the Burlington Police Department, this situation is not Waco, Texas. Tonight there'll be no mediators, exchange of demands or swat teams positioned on the rooftop of Nectar's Restaurant. The officer calls for back-up, and another cruiser — blue lights and all — pulls up in two minutes.

Both officers are a little peeved, because at this stage, I gather, paperwork comes into play. They put on latex gloves, and with well-choreographed positioning — this is by no means an unprecedented scenario for either of them — hoist my erstwhile customer out of the taxi and into the cruiser. Thankfully, at this moment of engagement, Joanie offers only token resistance.

At the end of the night, it's rare for me to second-guess myself. Experience has honed my instincts, and I think I handle myself pretty well out there. But tonight, as I pull to a stop, kill the ignition and turn off the taxi light, I wonder — could I have given Joanie a better shake?

Double Trouble

Incoming is a steady stream spread over six hours. The typical weekend night taxi trade begins around six with customers coming into town for an early movie or dinner, and continues through midnight with the late night bar revelers and music club aficionados.

Outgoing, by contrast, is a tsunami, a raging whitewater funneled through the solid hour signaled by last call. This is taxi rush hour, during which time the demand for cabs outstrips the supply of cabs. I live for taxi rush hour.

With dozens of people on the street hailing taxis, cabbies look to "double up". On one corner you pick up a couple heading to Williston; gaining their assent, you stop on the next corner and grab a guy going to the Sheraton. Such commingling of fares is both lucrative to the driver and of benefit to the public. Without doubling up, people would be stranded downtown scrambling to secure a cab ride home.

But here's the fly in the ointment. On rare occasions, two groups of people — finding themselves suddenly crammed together in a taxicab — commence to fight.

The rush is underway and two young men flag me down. They're both handsome, black-haired, strapping lads. Probably local guys back from college, or maybe a little older, I think.

"Where ya guys headed?" I call through the open window.

"Chase Lane," one replies, as he and his friend climb into the rear seat.

"Sounds good," I say. "Mind if I take another fare?"

"No problem — go for it, man."

Up the street, two young women are hailing me. They are both exceedingly attractive, though in very different ways. One of them is tall, willowy and of multi-race origin. The other has flashing black eyes, short auburn hair in a wide, violet bandanna, and she's wearing a halter top and tight jeans. She has the look and in-your-face demeanor of Rosie Perez, the terrific New York actress and choreographer of Puerto Rican heritage. When she speaks, sure enough, it is with that "Nuyorican" accent of a Latino New Yorker.

"You take us to Essex, man?" she asks. Then noticing the two guys in the back seat, "There's three of us, you know. We gawna fit?"

Standing on the curb is a hulk of a guy. He's beaming out a big smile, one of those immense, toothy jobs.

"No problem," I answer. "Two of you can get in the front and one in the back with the two guys. They're getting off at Chase."

The willowy woman gets in the back; "Rosie" squeezes in next to me, and then the big guy next to her. Visibly invigorated by the company of these good-looking women, one of the guys in the back attempts some conversation.

"You ladies from town or are you just visiting?"

Not turning to face the speaker, but speaking directly as if addressing the rear-view mirror, Rosie responds. As the words come out, she tilts her head a few degrees back and forth. This small pivot of the head is akin to a great fast ball pitcher adding a slight curve to the delivery: the fast ball alone is sufficient to achieve the strike out; the added curve says, "Not only do I get you, but I do so with panache."

"What's that? You tawkinuhme? You some kinda cool Vermont guy? Is that who you think you are?"

"Hey, what is your problem?" the guy says.

"So you think I gotta problem?" she says, turning to her friend in the back. "Ella, this guy here thinks I gotta problem. Do you think I gotta problem?"

I glance back at Ella, who looks like she wants to be anywhere but where she is at this moment. I don't think Rosie really expects an answer from her friend. It was what you call a "rhetorical question".

"What are you anyway?" The guy has been reduced to near sputtering. "The queen bitch from hell?"

"Are we angry, Vermont-boy? Whadaya gawna punch me?" She gestures to the big guy wedged to her right who looks like he has as much desire to play an active role in Rosie's drama as did Ella. "My boy here could kick your ass, and your friend's ass."

"Okay, let's go!" Vermont-boy has indeed lost it. "Pull over, cabbie. Right now — let's go!"

I am feeling a bunch of things at this moment. In an odd way, I'm truly impressed with Rosie — in awe really. In two compact minutes, she has evoked and delivered the energy of the *intefada* to our impromptu grouping. It's now open warfare in Jernigan-world. Mostly though, I'm freaked out. I am a Libra, the most Libra of Librans. I crave peace, harmony and equilibrium in my immediate surroundings. Like air, I crave it.

Under normal circumstances (ha!), I operate in the manner of a nursery school teacher who knows it's important for her wards to work out their conflicts with a minimum of outside intervention. But as commander of this vessel, I realize I had better do something quick before blows are thrown.

"Hey!" I say to Rosie. She ignores me totally. I squeeze her shoulder and she turns to face me. Our faces are 10 inches apart.

"Just because you have the power to get men angry doesn't mean you oughta. You're being very unfair. These two guys in the back are good guys. The one guy was just making friendly conversation."

"Yeah, that's right," the guy in the back says. He seems immensely relieved. He's just a good local kid. He didn't really want to fight the big guy in the front. It was just one of those gorilla-in-the-mist, male face-saving imperatives. "I was just trying to be nice."

I see Rosie's face change. A hardness, an anger drops from her cheeks and eyes. She's not that tough, really. It's an act — one she's nearly perfected, but an act nonetheless.

"Hey, you know what?" she says. "I don' even know what I said. I get in this car, I'm a little drunk — I didn' mean nothin'."

The back seat guy gets a big grin and says, "I didn't mean it either," and the two erstwhile antagonists exchange one of those slapping-soul handshakes that I can never execute quite right because, well frankly, I'm not that cool.

The remainder of the ride to Chase Lane becomes as chummy as the first few minutes were tension-packed. There's lots of laughing, flirting, good-natured ribbing — all-around bonhomie. As we stop to drop the two guys at their place, an elaborate exchange of phone numbers takes place. Who knows? Maybe the first part of the trip served an aphrodisiac function. Rosie's incitements certainly broke the ice, that's for sure.

The ride out to Essex continues in the affable motif so much easier on my frazzled nervous system. "Rosie" turns out to be Nicolette, Nicky for short, and she did grow up in New York City, coming up here to live with a favorite aunt who's working at IBM. Nicky's registered to begin at Champlain College later this summer.

"I care a lot about troubled kids, you know, so I wanna become a social worker," she tells me.

I think — and just barely manage to keep to myself — "Well, what a coincidence, Nicky. I am a social worker myself."

Submarine Warfare

When, as happens on occasion, I pick up a fare that results in a debacle of some sort, I get down on myself. I figure I've been at this for so long, I should have seen it coming. But as any veteran cabbie will tell you, sometimes you see it coming, and sometimes you don't.

It was the tail end of the Saturday night rush when I saw her out in the street, in front of the Kountry Kart Deli, flamboyantly flagging me down. When you're an attractive young woman wearing a sequined tube top and matching skirt, I suppose flamboyancy is what you're going for. She was hard to ignore: a white-wrapped sub sandwich tucked under one arm, the other arm flapping away like she was waving goodbye from the poop deck of the Queen Elizabeth.

She wavered in place like a bad gymnast on a balance beam. Maybe it was the strappy platform heels — in conjunction with whatever alcohol was downed during the course of the evening's festivities — compromising her stability.

It was here that the "seeing it coming" came and went. My hackie intuition said pass her by and pick up the two guys also looking for a cab on the corner by Manhattan Pizza. I think the sequins momentarily hypnotized me, clouding my judgment. (That could happen, right?) I stopped and she climbed in the front seat.

"Hey, dude," she said with a weary sigh. "This town is *crazy*. Get me outta here."

"Anywhere in particular?" I asked, the taxi still in park. I'm no martinet when it comes to taxi protocol, but there is one personal rule I hold inviolate: The cab doesn't go into drive until I hear an actual address.

"Henry Street, dude, take me to 3 Henry Street."

It's funny, I thought — I used to be a man; now I'm a dude. I don't know if that's a step up, down, or laterally.

Up Main Street we rolled. As I took a left onto Union she said, "Hey, what's this gonna run?"

"Four bucks."

"To Henry Street?" she barked. "That's, like, a rip-off, dude."

"Well, that's what it costs," I replied. "Tell me now. You wanna go back to the Kountry Kart?"

"No, just drive. I'll pay you."

I hate when customers grouse about the fares. I shouldn't, but I do. I know exactly what the fleets and other independents charge, and my rates are right in the ballpark — if not directly in the dugout — with my competitors. Still, it irks me.

Right on Pearl, left on Willard, and at Henry I took the right. "Stop right here," she said. "I'll run inside and get you the money."

"Wait a second," I said. "Why don't you leave something in the cab, so I know you're coming back?"

Now she turned to me, lowered her head and batted her eyes. "Seriously, dude, I'll come right down." She was suddenly speaking softly. "I don't have my purse with me; I have, like, nothing to leave with you."

Normally when a good-looking woman bats her eyes at me, she usually hits a home run. I'm that easy. Not this time, though.

"Leave the sub," I said.

"Seriously, I'm coming right back. I'm not leaving my sub." She had reverted to the not-so-nice speaking voice.

"Seriously," I replied, pointing to my head. "Do I have 'schmuck' written on my forehead? You know and I know you ain't comin' back once you get out of this taxi. Leave the sub."

She grabbed for the door handle, and as the door swung open, I lunged for the sub. In a pincers movement with my two hands, I latched onto one end, forestalling her escape. With the sub, anyway.

"Leggo my goddam sub!" she shrieked, pulling at the package from her end, one leg out of the vehicle, two in the morning, at 3 Henry Street.

"Just drop it and come back with the dough and it's yours," I countered, calmly. I'm great in a crisis.

She tugged; I maintained my grip. She relaxed for a moment, then tried a sneak yank, but I was not to be fooled.

Suddenly she gave a mighty jerk, and the sub slipped from her hands. She tumbled head over strappy heels onto Henry Street. Quickly popping up, her dignity — as well as mine, for that matter — out the window, she glared at me and yelled, "Idiot! Goddam Idiot!"

I looked back at her and just shrugged. She turned and hightailed it into her house. Although I knew it would be futile, I waited a good five minutes before taking off. Need I say she never came back?

This summer there's been a homeless guy who most nights hangs out at the corner of City Hall Park, by the taxi stand. He enjoys chewing the fat with us cabbies. When I got back downtown, I pulled up to him and called from the window.

"Hey, Larry," I said. "You hungry, tonight? Wanna unopened sub?"

I glanced down at the hard-won sandwich. It looked like it had been involved in a fight, which, of course, it had. "It's a wee bit mangled, but still fresh," I added, by way of full disclosure.

His eyes grew wide. "Sure, taximan," he replied. "You're all right, you know that?"

"No problem, Larry. Enjoy it." I passed him the sub through the window. "You know what, Larry? I won that sub in a tug of war."

Sexy Sadie

Sadie always comes out with a flourish. This time she was preceded by some hapless guy who hailed the cab for her in front of Esox. She emerged from the bar laughing uproariously and pointing back at a couple of men sitting on the bar stools that face out the bar's opened street front. Sadie is still young-girl sexy and flirtatious, though she must be pushing 35. And she still looks great — a minor miracle considering her years of club-hopping.

Holding open my rear door, the man called to her, "Hey, Sadie-girl — get your bad self in the cab."

"Thanks, darlin'," Sadie said, approaching the vehicle. Smiling at the man, she kicked closed the door he was holding open and unhurriedly let herself into the front seat with me.

"Let's do it, cabbie," she said, as her would-be escort stood there, drop-jawed.

"Okey-dokey," I said, and hit the accelerator.

"Do you believe that guy thought I'd go home with him? What a total loser! He *lives* at that friggin' bar. You know what they say: from Esox to detox."

"Where am I taking you, Sadie?" I asked.

"Meadow Run," she said. "You know where that is? Off 2A."

"Sure thing," I said, although I lose track of all those developments along 2A north of Taft's Corner. It's like new ones seem to appear overnight.

I glanced over and noticed Sadie was fiddling with the volume knob on the radio. The current top-40 hit by Uncle Kracker was playing. She succeeded in her aim, and now it was truly loud.

"Okay, if I turn up the music?" she asked, disingenuously, after the fact. She turned and looked at me wide-eyed, with her killer smile. This is a woman accustomed to getting her way with men, I thought, and I suppose I'm no exception.

"Sure," I said. "I like this tune. It's kinda shaping up as *the* summer song this year."

As we passed Chicken Charlie's, Sadie slid her seat way back, and put her sandaled feet up on the dash. "You don't mind?" she said, with a laugh. This is the deal, I gathered — you do it first, and ask questions later.

"Yeah, Sadie, just don't kick the steering wheel, all right?"

I knew she was playing me a little, but at this point of my life, I have no need to draw lines merely for the sake of "showing who's boss". From experience, I knew this to be Sadie's *modus operandi*, and so long as it didn't get out of hand, why stifle her?

"Cute hat," she said, snaring the baseball cap off my head and, in one fluid motion, placing it on her own. It looked so much better on her than me — but of course that would be true for any single article of clothing I was wearing.

"Whadaya think?" she said, in her best imitation of a New York accent. She had flipped the rear-view mirror in her direction, and was cracking herself up play-pouting, turning her head to and fro.

"Sadie, don't turn the mirror," I said, grabbing it and resetting the position so I could see what's coming up behind us. I don't think I spoke angrily, but as captain of this vessel, responsible for the safety of all passengers and crew, it was time to re-assert control.

"You're a friggin' spoil-sport," she yelled, throwing the hat into the back of the cab.

"Sadie, I need the mirror in place, that's all."

She sat there, now really pouting. At that moment, I felt like I was running a pre-school, which, come to think of it, is a fairly apt job description for a late-night hackie.

Arriving at the development, I said, "That'll be 10 bucks."

"Sorry, I only have three," Sadie replied. She yanked two crumpled singles from her tight jean pocket, threw them on the dash and got out of the cab. She was so confident and brazen. It wasn't like she was fleeing or even rushing.

At the same moment, her boyfriend emerged from the condo. He was bare-chested, and wearing only silk pajama bottoms. He was not a happy camper; he was not a happy puppy; he was not a happy anything. On the pathway to the front door, he intercepted and confronted Sadie. Despite the hour, he didn't even attempt to keep his voice down.

"So you finished your visit with Diane, I guess? Where the hell *were* you, Sadie? It's almost two in the morning, for Chrissake!"

"I was at Diane's," she replied, and blew past him disappearing into the condo.

The guy stood there for a good 20 seconds as I continued watching from my cab. His hands were on his hips, his head was bowed and the exasperation was written all over his body. He looked like he was either going to explode or burst into tears. Raising his head, he strode over to my window. I really didn't expect this; the cuckolded paramour generally maintains his privacy.

"Okay," he said, "where'd you pick her up?"

I hesitated for a moment before responding. Shall I tattle on Sadie?

"I picked her up at Esox, man."

Maybe if she had at least paid me the fare I would have owed her some discretion. Or maybe, I should have simply said, "You should talk to her about that," and taken off. Or maybe . . . any number of things.

'I knew it," he said, shaking his head, "I just knew it."

"How about paying the rest of the fare," I suggested. "She only gave me two bucks."

"Sure," he said. "I'll pay her fare. Just as soon as hell freezes over, brother." He then turned and walked away.

"Well then," I thought to myself, driving back into town for my next adventure, "that certainly went well."

Stewed Prune

Mr. Townsend met me at the door, shirttail hanging out, toothbrush tucked in his cheek. "Jernigan, hang out in the living room," he said, already turning his back on me to go up the stairs. "I'll be ready in a bit."

I shook my head, took a deep breath and strode into the big house. This was Warren, up near the Sugarbush ski slopes and the property could only be described as a small forest palace. Everything about the place screamed money, from the one-of-a-kind hand-carved dinner table to the four-car garage. I appreciate artful design in a home, but Mr. Townsend's Vermont get-a-way was neither graceful nor elegant. It struck me as ostentatious — wealth on display.

This customer always kept me waiting, and it drove me nuts. He was fanatical, even paranoid, about my getting there on time — sometimes calling two or even three times to confirm the pick-up. But when I arrived, he was never ready to leave. If he wasn't dressing, he was yelling into his cell phone at someone in a New York office. Most of the time he traveled by private jet, so departure times weren't set in stone; whenever we arrived at Burlington Airport, the pilots and plane would be waiting.

Worse than that, half the time he wouldn't have money on him, like he was the Queen of England or something. "I'll get you next time" was the refrain. He always made good, but sometimes it would be weeks.

So I sat stewing in the living room, ensconced in a big, plump, purple chair. I think the interior decorator might have intended a post-modern nod to the classic La-Z-Boy, but to actually sit in the thing was like being embraced by a giant prune.

After the better part of a half-hour, Mr. Townsend popped into view, smiling vividly if not manically. The guy is so tightly wired, I've actually wondered if he's a cokehead. I know he's a partner in a Wall Street law firm specializing in corporate takeovers, so cocaine would not be out of the question. Pirates guzzled rum, after all, to fuel their dirty deeds.

"Let's do it," he said. "Let's go, go, go." In his left hand he held the omni-present laptop, in the right a small gym bag. I think he maintains a complete set of clothes up here, one in his New York City apartment and another at the law office. It's really a snap: every time you purchase an article of clothing, you simply say to the clerk, "Make it three."

We cruised along Route 100, passing Harwood Union High School and Lots o' Balls mini-golf. It took lots o' balls to come up with that name, I thought to myself. As we drove along, Mr. Townsend received and initiated a series of cell calls, and with each successive call he grew more agitated. His half of the last conversation was straight out of the Sopranos.

"We'll bury him. Ya understand? He's dead. Dead man walking. This deal is happening; end of story. He thinks — what? — he's gonna screw us in the eleventh hour? He won't know what hit him, like an alligator on a fucking poodle. That goes for the whole board, if they stick with this moron. The blood will flow like blood. You saw the first 10 minutes of *Saving Private Ryan*? That's what I'm talking about."

I glanced up at the rearview to see Mr. Townsend shaking a Lucky Strike out of the pack. Yes, I let him smoke in the cab, just one of many compromises I've made to maintain this steady, lucrative fare.

"Ya know what?" he said, apropos of nothing. "It's not about 'greed is good.' That misstates it." He inhaled with a vengeance, drawing the essence of Lucky Strike deep into his lungs. "It's inserting a moral judgment where none is called for. Greed is reality. It isn't 'good'; it isn't 'bad'. It's air."

Mr. Townsend, I knew from experience, was not remotely interested in my reaction to this thesis; in his world, I'm wallpaper on wheels. But I was glad he said what he said, because in that moment I made my decision.

We reached the private plane terminal, and Mr. Townsend snapped the computer back into its case. He said, "Good news — I have some money on me. I owe you for last trip too, correct?"

"Yup, you sure do."

He handed me the money and said, "I probably won't be back up until after the holidays. I'll call you then."

"Don't," I said.

"Whaddaya mean, 'don't'?" He looked both puzzled and irked.

"Sorry, but I'm not driving you anymore, Mr. Townsend, so you'll have to call some other company."

"Are you kidding me?! What's this about?"

"Oh, it's hard to say, really. Let's just say I'm moving on."

"I don't know what the fuck your problem is." He was glaring at me with such venom, for a moment I felt like dead man driving.

"I don't know what my problem is either, man." Just before he slammed the door, I added, "The thing is, it might not even be a problem."

Not Getting Killed

"Yo, cabby! Over here!"

I turned my head to the left and caught sight of the raised, out-stretched arm. Said arm — massive and muscled — was attached to an equally impressive male body. Both arm and body stood across Main Street on the curb by City Hall Park. Positioned next to this vision of male pulchritude stood a woman. I pulled to my right, put on the four-ways, and waited for the two of them to cross Main Street and get into my taxi.

Downtown was busy this Friday night, so I had the chance to observe the couple as they waited for a break in the traffic. The woman was strikingly beautiful, and with her height, I thought could well be a model. She wore a black mini-dress, and had bobbed auburn hair which highlighted her large, wide-set dark eyes. The entire effect was not so much va-va-voom as entirely cute, completely adorable. She was also, I could tell as I watched her, very drunk; she listed slowly to and fro as her companion held onto her arm in an attempt to maintain her in a position relatively perpendicular to the earth. With some effort, they made it across to my cab.

"Go ahead, honey. Get on in. I'll meet you back at the room in a little while," the man said as he opened the rear door with one hand and continued to steady the woman with the other.

"But I don't want to miss any of the fun," she said in a plaintive, sing-song voice. It was clear this was no serious disagreement, just a cutesy *pas de deux*.

"Don't worry, babe, you won't miss a thing; I'll be back before you know it," he said easing her into the seat and closing the door behind her. He then turned to speak to me through my open window.

"How much to take her to the Radisson?"

"That would be four bucks."

"Okay," he said, removing a twenty from his wallet and handing it to me. "It's all yours, but I want you to see her into the hotel and up to her room."

"Buddy," I replied glancing at the new, big-head Thomas Jefferson twenty, "for this tip I'll do that, plus shine your shoes and wax your car. He-heh."

That's me, I thought, the master of the quick-witted, good-natured cabbie comeback.

I looked up at him with a goofy grin, and watched as — right before my eyes — his lips grew thin and hard, and his pale, blue eyes slowly turned, God help me, to a piercing, steely gray. He narrowed those eyes and focused them on me like two gamma rays. This is what he then said to me, ver-frigging-batim: "If you touch her, I will find you, and I will kill you."

I gulped. My goofy grin wavered. I suddenly felt very light-headed, the result perhaps of all the blood draining from my face. For the life of me, I could not think of any possible reply. Those crafty Frenchmen have an expression: "*esprit d'escalier*", meaning "clever repartee one thinks of too late". But now weeks later I still can't come up with anything. How about, "Don't fret — I won't be touching her, so you needn't be concerned about tracking me down and killing me?" I don't think so.

Confident that his little warning had achieved the desired effect — i.e. completely freaking me out — the guy nodded, smiled slightly and sauntered back across the street. I took three deep yoga breaths, and turned around to see how the woman in the back had taken the chummy exchange I had just had with her boyfriend. She shot me a mile-wide smile that registered total obliviousness. She had made herself comfortable back there, laying out on the back seat like it was a lounge chair on a cruise ship. The dress, which was astoundingly short to begin with — let's say PG-13 — had entered NC-17 territory.

"Home, James!" she said, and began giggling. "You know, Mr. Cabbie, I always wanted to say that — and now — I've said it!" The hilarity of that thought cracked her up yet further.

All right: to the Radisson, check; help her out of the cab, check; see her through the lobby, into the elevator, and to her room — check, check, check. Piece o' cake. Except how on God's green earth will I accomplish this without touching her? She's exceedingly wobbly; shan't I take her arm?

This is a touchy subject. Logically, of course, the guy meant "touch" as in getting your jollies, and not merely "touch" of the helpful variety. But are these not sometimes fine judgment calls? There's a lot at stake here, namely my hide. I'm not that young anymore, I thought, but still too young to die.

"I don't want to go to the Radisson. Let's go to Montreal, Mr. Cabbie. What do you say? Let's have some fun." She was now bouncing up and down, like her seat was a small trampoline.

"I don't think so, ma'am. I think getting you back to your room is the best choice right now."

"Ma'am? Give me a freakin' break! My name is Donna." She flashed me a big, crooked smile that was, like everything else about her, too cute for words.

"Okay Donna," I said, not really wanting to be on a first-name basis. But what could I do? I'm Mr. Cabbie and she's Donna. "Here's the Radisson; let's get you up to your room safe and sound."

I helped her out of the cab, and walked her through the lobby as she held my arm. I kept up this inner mantra: *I am the boy scout and she is the granny . . . I am the boy scout and she is the granny.* The elevator arrived and together we stepped in. She showed me her room key which indicated which floor button to press.

As we lifted off, bound for the sixth floor, she leaned her back against the wall, interlaced her fingers and slowly raised her hands to the back of her head. I was whistling "Crimson and Clover" by Tommy James and the Shondells, because that was playing on the radio on the ride over, and I was focusing — to the best of my ability — on the lighted floor indicator above the door. This is the slowest elevator in the Western world, I thought. Maybe the elevator is slower in the Sheraton Ho Chi Minh City, but in the industrialized world, this puppy has got to be the slowest. Through the corner of my eye, I mean the tiniest peripheral sliver, I noticed that those wide, dark eyes were staring at me.

"You know something, Mr. Cabbie? You look awfully cute with that Vermont baseball cap. Do you know that?"

I felt the life force ebbing away. "Go into the light, Jernigan; go into the light." But I want to live! I want to live! In a rush, I felt the life force surge back into my body.

"No, Donna," I said, "that's where you couldn't be more wrong." For the first time I looked directly at her, right into her eyes. "I'm not handsome; I'm not hunky; I'm not hot. And one thing for damn sure: I'm not in the least bit cute. What I am is probably old enough to be your father."

Her eyes and face relaxed into a sweet, innocent smile. I smiled back. The elevator stopped and I helped her to her room. She said thanks, and I left.

And that was how I survived to live and breathe for another day.

Instant Karma

"Do you believe in retribution?"

These words, this question, was the first utterance delivered by the fortyish man I picked up on a chilly December night. As he entered the cab, my usual prompt — "Anywhere in particular" — fell on deaf ears. Hearing no response, I turned in my seat to rephrase the question, perhaps this time minus the would-be wit. His countenance, however, rendered me dumbstruck. He sat there with a glazed-over look in his eyes. His demeanor evinced spaciness, disassociation, intoxication or some combination of the three. Still, I sensed purpose in the dazed reverie — a focus of mind scary in its resolution. His presence left me frozen.

Finally, after what seemed like a minute, his asked the retribution question again, breaking our silent stand-off. The transformation was disarming: one second out to lunch; the next piercingly present. The switch startled me, to say the least, and I am not one of delicate sensibility. I might even have visibly trembled at the sound of his voice. It was like the precise moment when day turns to night, and the sleeping vampire springs upright in the coffin, opens wide his eyes and looks right at you.

I was hoping, praying really, that the question was rhetorical, because I truly did not want to engage in a discussion with this guy — not even about the weather, let alone on the subject of retribution.

No such luck. He repeated for the third time, albeit with a modicum less intensity, "Do you believe in retribution?"

I said, "Let me think about that one a minute. In the meantime, would you tell me where we're going?"

"Sure," he said, and gave me a location in the New North End. "It'll be round-trip."

Turning onto Battery Street and heading north, I relaxed somewhat. I always feel better when the taxi is in drive.

"To answer your question," I said, "I don't believe in retribution. My experience has shown that what goes around, comes around. It's not for me to dole out punishment, however deserving the recipient. It's just not my job, and besides, when I've tried it, it just ups the ante and comes back to me double."

"That's an interesting perspective," he said. "But what if a man stole your wife. Would you still feel that way?"

The whole discussion was beginning to take a "Pulp Fiction-esque" turn. The original and compelling conceit of that movie was the specter of two cold-blooded hit men engaged in philosophical debates in between, and sometimes during, their nefarious assignments. Here's what scared me about the situation at hand: (a) the subtext that this was somehow not a purely intellectual discussion, in conjunction with (b) this wasn't a movie.

Why couldn't I cut the discussion short? Everything about this inter-action was disturbing; where was my cabdriver savvy? The whole thing was beginning to feel like a run-away train.

I plunged ahead. "Well, I've never had a wife who was stolen, so it's hard to say how I'd react. Still, I think revenge is not solution." Brilliant, huh?

"Well," he said. "I beg to differ."

Thank goodness he said no more. We pulled up to his destination, a modest single-family home, and he said to wait a minute as he'd be right back. I watched him stride to the front door and knock forcefully. No one responded. He next walked around to peer through some windows. Only a couple of lights in the house were on; presumably no one was home. He returned to the taxi and got back in the rear seat.

"Do you have a small piece of paper and a pen?" he asked.

"Will a business card work?" I said.

"Yes it will," he said, and he reached for the card and pen I offered. He then paused. "Actually, could you write it for me? I'm in no shape to write tonight."

"Okay," I said. "Whadaya want me to say?" I thought, will the fun never stop?

"Write, 'Don't fuck with me'," he dictated.

Recognizing I was past the point of no return — that boat having sailed way earlier in this junket — I faithfully inscribed the inspirational message he requested, and gingerly handed it over. He re-exited the vehi-cle, walked over to the Ford Explorer parked in the driveway and placed the card on the windshield under a wiper.

By this point, I'd placed myself on a strictly need-to-know basis, so the lack of conversation on the return trip was a godsend. I glanced at my passenger once in the rear-view, and he was doing the glazed-over thing again. I decided that's the way I liked him better. Back downtown, he quietly paid and was gone. As I pulled back into traffic, a Dave Mamet line popped into my head: "That was more fun than a fuckin' aquarium."

The following afternoon, the Burlington Police called and asked me to "please" come to the station. The Sergeant said he'd tell me what it's about when I got there. Great.

At he police station, I was led into a small room, the Sergeant across the desk. "Is this your business cart?" he asked, handing me the card from last night with the lovely sentiment on the back.

"It sure is," I replied, and proceeded to relate the entire incident from the previous night. It came out only slightly less convoluted than the story of Alice's Restaurant.

The Sergeant listened intently, and when I was finally done, said, "We know all about this guy. This is his second violation of the ex-wife's restraining order. He's going to jail."

"Just don't tell me I'll have to testify," I said.

"Highly unlikely, Mr. Pontiac," he replied. "I think we have all the evidence we need."

One good thing about hacking — whatever happens, you're soon back in the taxi, rolling along, with plenty of time for processing the experience. John Lennon, I reflected, had it right about so many things: "Instant karma's gonna get you. Gonna knock you off your feet."

4

Beyond the City Limits

I'm a city cabbie. In the greater scheme of things, Burlington, Vermont,
with fewer than 40,000 residents, is a small city, but in the context of a
state that remains largely rural, Burlington is the cultural and economic hub.
Most of my fares begin and end within Burlington and the circle of
surrounding towns. On occasion, however, and particularly during
foliage season, I catch a fare that takes me out of the city, and into
the sylvan beauty of the Green Mountains.

Vermont Dreaming

She looked to be on the elderly side of middle-aged, broad faced, plain brown hair pulled back. It was last spring, late April or early May. As we left the Essex Junction Amtrak station in my taxi heading west towards the lake, I thought, *this woman looks like an Andrew Wyeth model, but from the Midwest.*

Passing the Fort and St. Michael's College, we chatted easily and I quickly surmised that Anna was just that — a lifetime Okie on her first trip east of the Mississippi. She expressed a keen interest in seeing the Green Mountains "close-up." I offered my taxi and myself as, respectively, tour bus and tour guide, and Anna heartily accepted. Pick-up time was set for noon the following day. I told her to plan for a three-hour tour. Unlike the ill-fated *Minnow* on "Gilligan's Island," I told her my tours come with a no-shipwreck guarantee. She laughed and told me I was a "great kidder".

Heading for bed that night, I eagerly anticipated the next day's trip. About once a month, more in the foliage season, I catch a tour like this. It's good money, it breaks up the monotony of the in-town grind, and I'm not so Vermont-jaded that I don't appreciate getting into the hills, trees and fields for a few hours. As an added incentive, not that I needed it, the Notch had just opened up, and springtime in Stowe just kills me.

I figured I'd give her the standard loop: covered bridge in Jeff, up over the Notch, Trapp Family Lodge, and maybe finish up at my favorite tourist trap, the Cold Hollow Cider Mill. But as I was to find out, there was nothing standard about Anna's life. This trip, moreover, represented nothing less then the crowning fulfillment of her life's journey.

The next day was glorious. The sky was Aqua Velva, the sun warm and lemony, with just the slightest tickle of a breeze. Anna was waiting at the front of the hotel, and jumped right into the seat next to me. She was wearing a frock and beaming.

We rolled down Route 15, me the consummate tour guide. All that was missing was one of those handheld microphones. "Yup, this is Jericho, home of the improbable Snowflake Bentley." What I didn't know, I made up, and Anna ate up every hokey detail. As we cruised onto the Pleasant Valley Road through Underhill, I finally shut up and asked her about her life. Her plainspoken sincerity hit me in the heart.

Her dad's farm failed during the dust bowls of the '30's, she told me, and the family was left destitute. It was just as chronicled by John Steinbeck or Woody Guthrie except Anna's family didn't leave for California but stayed on in Oklahoma as itinerant farm workers. By age eight or nine, she was pitching in.

Packing strawberries one lonely summer day, she slipped a note with her name and address into the bottom of a container, a "message in a bottle". Later that summer she received a letter from one Georgia Littlefield, a 10 year-old Nebraska schoolgirl, and, yes, she would "love" to be her pen pal. It would be "swell".

From this unlikeliest of beginnings arose a lifelong friendship of the utmost intimacy. Anna and Georgia shared each other's lives from the teen years into adulthood. On rare occasions there were visits, but mostly they communicated through letters, and, later, by telephone. And one thing they shared was an enchantment with Vermont.

They both subscribed to *Vermont Life* and would read every article religiously. Every so often *National Geographic* would do a feature on maple syruping, ice fishing or skiing, and they would clip the pictures scrapbook-style. I asked Anna how two born-and-bred Midwestern farm girls came to hear about Vermont, let alone develop an utter enthrallment with this most Yankee of northeastern states.

"I can't honestly recall," she replied. "From my earliest childhood, I would imagine a land of tall hills, white snow and deep green forests. I didn't take long before Georgia — bless her heart — was sharing the same dream."

At the long covered bridge just outside of Jeffersonville village, Anna handed me her camera and had me shoot any number of pictures of her waving, throwing pebbles into the stream below, and, in her own demure way, generally vamping it up. Getting into the spirit of the occasion, I told her she looked better than Meryl Streep in *The Bridges of Madison County*. She blushed, said she had seen the movie, but just knew that Vermont's covered bridges would outclass anything that Clint Eastwood could come up with. Now she knew she was right.

As we passed the Smuggler's Notch ski lifts and began the sharp ascent through the Notch itself, Anna was visibly transported. She looked like a kid on her first visit to an old-fashioned candy store. A few pockets of snow still dotted the cliff side. Here and there roadside waterfalls gushed cool, clear water through crevices that looked like laugh lines on the faces of kindly old men.

We stopped at one of the many pullovers near the peak so Anna could wander a little and take some photos. I glanced at her face as I walked nearby. It was as if she was imprinting this wondrous vista for all time, storing it forevermore in her mind's eye.

On the Stowe side heading towards the Trapp place, Anna spoke more of her friend Georgia. They had both married in their twenties. Georgia had two children, now both middle-aged themselves. She herself was childless. They both were widowed relatively young, in their fifties. Though she spoke in no specifics, I read between the lines that neither she nor her friend had any money to speak of.

Always, through the years, they planned their trip to Vermont, just the two of them. "But one thing leads to another," she said, "and you know how it is. A few years ago Georgia developed a serious heart problem. Now she couldn't possibly make the journey."

I looked over and could see the pain on her face.

"But you know," she continued, quickly perking up, "Georgia practically forced me to go on this trip. Do you believe it, age 74, never traveled a whit, and now here I am, seeing Vermont for the both of us."

The panorama from the Trapp Family Lodge is simultaneously vast and intimate. If there's a beating heart to the Green Mountains, I think it's here in these rolling alpine fields. Just one look, and there's no doubt why Maria plopped her intrepid family right down at this spot. At the Lodge's terrific gift shop, Anna bought a comically large number of postcards — mostly black and white reproductions of early Vermont scenes.

"Georgia will just eat these up," she said.

Down Route 100 into Waterbury Center, and the Cold Hollow Cider Mill was surprisingly quiet, even for this late, mud-season weekday. The place is run by a direct descendant of Vermont's first governor, and that's just one of the store's charming aspects. It's the opposite of slick, just stacks upon rows of gorgeous Vermont-made crafts and foods in no discernable order.

We bought a few cider donuts and two cups of fresh cider, and stepped outside to relax on a wooden bench under a maple tree. I glanced over and Anna was glowing. I imagined this was the demeanor of a practicing Muslim who has finally made it to Mecca, or a devout Jew praying for the first time at the Western Wall. Her eyes were at once a million miles away and almost jarringly present. She was 74 years old, wearing a shapeless dress of some unrecognizable flower motif, and all I can say is, she looked beautiful.

She turned and looked at me straight on. "Vermont is everything I always imagined," she said. "Never will I forget this day."

On the way back to Burlington, we spoke little. Camel's Hump is a palpable presence along the stretch from Waterbury to Burlington. On that afternoon it felt like a mammoth and friendly great-uncle watching over us. Donning my tour guide's hat for a final time, I told Anna that "Camel's Hump" is a fine descriptive name for this peak, but the hikers' had a nickname which I felt more truly captured the spirit of the mountain — "The Crouching Lion".

As with just about every aspect of this magical day, Anna found this perfect. "The Crouching Lion", she said, "is just about the cat's pajamas."

Back at the hotel, it was hard for me to say goodbye. Anna couldn't have been more gracious. She gave me a nice tip and had the bellhop take a few photos of the two of us standing alongside the taxi. She assured me she would keep my card for "the next time", and warmly shook my hand. We both knew there would be no next time. It was bittersweet.

It's been quite a few months since my time with Anna. Spring has long since blossomed into full-blown summer, and already the opening notes of the autumn symphony have been struck. Before you know it, the leafers will be arriving by the busload. Who can begrudge the tourists their infatuation with the blazing glory of fall foliage? For some, however, the attraction to Vermont goes far deeper.

Now looking back, I see that Anna taught me a soul lesson, a lesson in gratitude. Just as we often take for granted the loved ones most close to us, I forget the everyday blessing of life in Vermont. Why do I, and not Anna, get to call the Green Mountains my home? These are matters of fate and spirit I wouldn't even pretend to fathom. But of one thing I have no doubt: if where we get to live was determined by pure, unaffected desire, Anna would settled here long ago.

I can close my eyes and picture one Oklahoma-born farm girl. There's light in her eyes, and the wind is blowing through her soft brown hair. She's spending all her days whispering and laughing with her best friend, running through the fields of the Crouching Lion.

Chocolate River

It was a slow weeknight when I received the call to deliver a piece of lost airline luggage up to Smuggler's Notch. It was a welcome piece of work: the early spring weather was calm — no hint of precipitation — and I never tire of the trip up Route 15. I generally take the Pleasant Valley Road through Underhill Center, which puts you right into downtown Jeffersonville. From there it's just the short hop up the Mountain Road to the ski area. No muss; no fuss.

Through the years, I've driven many a tourist to Smuggs, hence I'm quite familiar with the resort "village". This bag was bound for the Sterling Ridge condo units, a name I didn't recognize. Probably new construction, I thought; the front desk would give me directions when I get there.

The drive up was uneventful, but that's not to say unpleasant. It was one of those crisp, clear night skies, the Milky Way all ablaze. The Red Sox were blowing an early-season game, but win or lose, it was wonderfully soothing to have baseball back on the radio. The voice of the play-by-play man over the dull roar of the crowd is, to me, like a rattle to a baby. All in all, I was quite the happy cabbie.

In about 40 minutes, I turned left into the Village at Smuggler's Notch. I pulled up to the Welcome Center, walked in and jauntily stepped up to the desk.

"Hey there," I greeted the two front desk people, a young man and woman. They each wore long-sleeved, purple polo shirts emblazoned with the Smuggler's Notch logo. "Could you tell me where the Sterling Ridge units are?"

The woman said, "Do you have an S.U.V.?"

"No," I replied. "I sure don't." This is not a good question, I thought.

The man said, "Do you have heavy-duty winter tires?"

"Okay," I said, "now you got me nervous. I have a regular American car with semi-crappy tires. Just where are these units?"

"The Sterling Ridge condos are up Edwards Road, a few miles past the Red Fox Inn," the woman said. "Do you know where that is?"

"Yeah, I think so." Edwards road runs north off Route 108, a couple miles before you hit Smuggs. What had been a jolly evening was turning sour. This is where I got a tad sarcastic, as if the placement of these condos was the ill-advised decision of these two people.

"That sure ain't in the 'village'," I pointed out. "I thought the whole point of the 'village' concept was setting all the units within walking distance of the lifts. It seems these Sterling Ridge condos have been banished from the 'village', wouldn't you say?"

I thought that was pretty funny, but I could tell from their eye-rolling that I was alone on that. Maybe it wasn't actually funny, now that I think about it; maybe it was passive-aggressive. In any event, I plunged ahead.

"I take it the road is in rough shape."

"Yeah, it's pretty soupy," the man replied.

"Well," I said. "I got this delivery up there, and I'm like the Post Office: neither snow, nor sleet, nor soup will stop me." I turned and walked out; in my last over-the-shoulder glimpse of them, I saw they were doing the eye-rolling thing again.

Here's a fact that's rarely recognized: there is no mud season in Burlington. Not really. It's a reality I often forget because — despite the occasional out-of-town fare — I'm essentially an urban cabdriver. It's another example of the truth in what rural Vermonters say about this city: the great thing about Burlington is that it's so close to Vermont.

Edwards Road is a dirt road. At its beginning, the mud appeared only a couple of inches thick, yielding a path of some solidity and traction. As it wended onward and upward, that didn't last. The ubiquitous ruts softened up, entered a gelatinous stage, and then were swallowed up entirely. The mud became thick, oozy, primal, primordial. In the chalky moonlight, the road glistened, moist and alive.

I pushed ahead at a steady pace — too much speed and I'd spin out of control; too little and I'd grind to a halt and sink slowly into the netherworld. It's just like the rapids, I thought: Once you've entered, it's do or die, no turning back.

Hands to the tiller, my mind riveted with piercing intensity on the next 10 yards, the next 10 yards, the next 10 yards. The front bumper split turbulent waves of brown muck. In stretches, the stuff crested the bottom of the windows. Small stones clicked and clacked against the undercarriage.

A steely determination came upon me as a physical force, as if by dint of will alone I could propel the vehicle to Sterling Ridge. Around a wide turn, the hallucinations began. On my driver's side, I saw the rounded hump of one of those new VW bugs bulge from the surface; off to the right, the antlers of a bull moose extended through the mud pack. It occurred to me that I was now fully prepared for a murky death; if this be the final fare, I'll go down proudly — in the driver's seat, hands firmly on the wheel. *Sic Transit Gloria Hackie.*

Then, in the near distance, I beheld the gabled roofs of what I mightily hoped were the Sterling Ridge condos. They seemed to beckon to me, to send me strength. I thought maybe, just maybe, I can make it through.

Taking the final turn, I came upon the thickest section yet. I confronted — to my fascination and horror — the mother of all muddy roads, a bubbling, undulating wall of mire. This had to be the Earth energy incarnate; if we were in Hawaii, there would be a Goddess appellation for this awesome, awful wonder: Mukaleela Lavahoha, or something like that.

Out loud — maybe to Mukaleela — I spoke a prayer. I straightened up in the seat, slunk the transmission into low gear, and gunned it. I hit the wall and entered that underworld I so feared. For what seemed like a short lifetime, but was probably five seconds, I saw nothing but brown, the only light a faint, green glow off the instrument panel. Then the engine screamed, and I burst through — thrust back to the land of the living.

The ground was level and relatively firm. I eased to a stop and took a deep breath. Glancing to my right, I broke out in a smile that went ear-to-ear. In the gleaming moonlight, the wood-carved sign read, "Sterling Ridge".

I stepped out of the taxi, gingerly unfolding my frame for a major stretch. Straightening up, I took a long, appreciative gander at my now mud-encased vehicle. It wasn't designed for sport or utility, I thought, but it sure got the job done.

Being With Jackie

Jackie is a tiny woman, not quite five feet, with short black hair beginning to show gray. She is vivacious, warm and uncommonly inquisitive.
Northern Pennsylvania is her home, just below Elmira, New York. Every
year she summers at her parents' camp in Milton, on a quiet, wind-swept
cove — the site of perhaps a dozen rustic cottages, all within 20 yards of
the shoreline. Some of the houses have stood for over 100 years; it's said
that these are the oldest collection of summer camps on the Vermont side
of Lake Champlain.

For many years, I have transported Jackie back and forth, to and from
her summer residence. It's a long haul, usually seven to eight hours each
way, depending on the number of rest stops taken. Certainly it would take
less time to make the journey by air, but for Jackie that would be far too
complicated and hectic. Jackie is developmentally disabled, what was once
called retarded; her mental capacity is that of a seven year-old. Traveling in
my taxi is a safe, pleasant routine for her.

Jackie's mother, Faith Reynolds, is a Vermonter down to her very soul.
She was born and grew up in Proctor. Her marriage in the early '30's to a
flatlander entailed settling in upstate New York. But her husband had a
great love for Vermont, and in the early years of their marriage they purchased the summer camp in Milton. If they couldn't make Vermont their
permanent home, at least they would visit every vacation. The passing of
her husband in the late '70's has not altered the routine: Faith has continued her summer pilgrimage to Lake Champlain without fail.

Faith is now 91 years-old. Her eyes glow with the intensity of a
teenager, indicative of a still sharp, probing mind. Like her daughter, she
lives out-of-state during the non-summer months, in a condo on Florida's
gulf coast. I drive Faith from the airport when she flies up to Burlington.
When I'm with her, I have no sense of being with the ancient person that

she is; if anything, she is more engaging than the vast majority of people I know, of whatever age.

Like most old folks, Faith loves to reminisce about the "old days", and I eat up these stories with a spoon. But unlike a lot of older people, she is as interested in the lives and stories of others. She's an avid listener, and year after year I'm flabbergasted at her accurate recall of various details of my life. She never fails to express her appreciation for my taxi service. "Jackie likes driving with you, you know" she told me in one of our conversations. "Why every spring, during our phone chats, she always asks, 'Jernigan will be driving me this year, right Mommy? Remember to call him, now.'"

Faith had been ailing this spring, experiencing an unaccustomed instability, bordering some days on real dizziness. She came up to camp on schedule in early June, but there was a question of whether her health would permit Jackie to join her. By July, however, perhaps buoyed by Vermont itself, she was feeling perkier, and she telephoned to arrange an early August pick-up of Jackie. It would be a short visit this year for her daughter, just a few weeks.

On the appointed day, I left Burlington at seven in the morning, and arrived at the Martha Lewis Home just before two. Jackie was waiting in the office, suitcase packed, with Teddy in his usual backpack traveling quarters. My heart rose when I spotted her; she's really an old friend at this point.

With a shout of, "You're here!", Jackie came towards me, arms outstretched. She's not one for holding back her feelings, particularly affection. Because she's so diminutive, her hug is like a wisp. In feeling quality, however, it's no less than a bear hug.

"C'mon, Jernigan," she said. "See my friends." She took my hand and led me into a large wood frame building adjacent to the office. We walked together through a double set of swinging doors, and into a room where a dozen or more middle-aged women sat busily engaged in painting, cutting, pasting and the like. For an instant, I was back in summer camp, stringing lariat key chains from long, brightly colored, vinyl twine.

"Hey, Jackie," the young attendant called from the far side of the room. "We thought you'd left already."

Jackie looked toward the attendant, but did not respond. She didn't so much introduce me around, as simply lead me into the center of the room in show-and-tell fashion, minus the "tell". I was roundly ignored, except for one woman with brassy, red bushy hair, who bounded up to me dangling a beaded wooden necklace of glossy primary colors.

"I'm Addie," she bellowed. "Look what I made." I told her it was lovely.

Mission accomplished, Jackie instructed me, "Let's go, Jernigan." Once on the road, Jackie's distress over her mother's condition was evident.

"Is Mommy better now? Jo-Jo (which is what she calls herself) was scared, almost couldn't come to Vermont this year."

As she spoke these words, her clear blue eyes shone with the deepest mixture of love and concern. Jackie is a person with no discrepancy between her heart and speech; there is no shading, strategy or agenda. This is one reason why I enjoy being with her. I assured her that her mom was feeling much better and couldn't wait to see her. With that, she visibly relaxed and settled in for the long journey.

After eating the bag lunch they had sent her with — an egg salad sandwich (her absolute favorite), a can of Pepsi, and a cookie — it was time for our first of many rest stops. Outside Cooperstown, New York, I glided off the highway up to one of the ubiquitous gas stations, and helped Jackie out of the seat belt, always a tricky maneuver for her. She stepped out of the car and held my hand as we slowly walked together into the store. She stopped in front of the counter facing the clerk and said, "Hello, how are you?" She never fails to greet the storekeepers. By her demeanor and slightly slurred speech, Jackie is clearly identifiable as a developmentally disabled person. The clerk, an older woman, responded, "Why thank you, dear. I'm just fine."

I learn a lot from Jackie's communication with these strangers. She's not in the least bit pushy, inappropriate nor loud. Her style is direct and open. This quality of unmistakable authenticity touches most everyone with whom she interacts.

Back in the taxi, rolling down Interstate 88, I noticed Jackie's eyes had suddenly grown wide. Every trip there is something that seems to rivet Jackie's attention. This time it was the yellow diamond, deer crossing signs.

"We didn't see any deer yet," she said. "Where are the deer, Jernigan? When are we going to see the deer?" As far as she was concerned, the deer signs meant we were going to see deer. I grasped her drift, and attempted to carefully spell out the point of these signs.

"It's like this, Jackie — you very seldom actually see any deer. The signs are erected by the highway department so drivers won't be startled if they do see a deer on the roadway. This way fewer deer are hit by cars."

I could see Jackie was looking at me intently, taking in every word of my clever explanation. Then ensued a few moments of silence followed by, "Okay, when are we going to see the deer, Jernigan?"

Miles before Albany, Jackie began asking, about every 15 minutes, "Are we in Vermont yet, Jernigan?" When we at last crossed over the bridge on Route 4, outside of Fairhaven, I pointed out the "Welcome to Vermont" sign, and said, "We're in Vermont now, Jackie." For Jackie, it was like V-Day in Times Square.

"We're in Vermont now, Jernigan!," she bubbled over. "Jo-Jo is in Vermont!"

It was half past nine when we pulled up the long, gray gravel driveway and eased to a stop in front of the Reynolds family camp. Faith came out the front porch door, eyes beaming with love. Jackie got out of the cab and unexpectedly began wailing, tears streaming down her face. With all her tiny frame, she embraced her mother.

"Mommy, I was so scared," she sobbed. "But you're not sick anymore, right?"

"Now Jackie, you promised no tears," Faith spoke as she hugged and patted Jackie again and again on her back. "You just calm down now. Everything is all right, dear."

"We made it here this summer," Jackie said, now with a big smile. "We made it, didn't we Mommy?"

Exhausted after 17 hours of straight driving, I headed back to Burlington. I stuck to Route 7; I couldn't bear to get back on the highway again. My thoughts drifted back to Jackie and the way she relates with the people in her life.

I thought of the mother-daughter reunion I had just witnessed. Jackie's expression of her deepest feelings of fear, sorrow and ultimately joy, flowed from the depth of her heart with purity and directness. As a person confounded daily, it seems, by the challenge of merely recognizing, let alone sharing my emotions, I was profoundly moved by Jackie's exchange with her mother. I contemplated the layers of filter, doublethink and flat-out repression that seems to permeate my emotional life.

I can't imagine a life without an adult intellect, and the responsibilities, joys and woes which flow therefrom. But Jackie has something which I don't, or perhaps it's something I once had but then lost: Jackie has an innocent heart.

Hunka-Hunka

Some men got it. Denzel Washington — so say the women in my life — has it. The guy sitting next to me, as we depart the Radisson on a foliage tour, does not have it. His name is Stan; he's middle-aged; he's lumpy; and he's the general sales manager of the second largest Ford dealership in Illinois. His boss — and that would be the owner of the second largest Ford dealership in Illinois — sits in the rear seat. His name is Brandt and he has it.

Perhaps because I am heterosexual, I have the darnedest time ascertaining the relative sex appeal of men. For instance, though I'm told women dearly appreciate a "good set of buns", this only begs the question of what makes for a "good set". You could line up facing backwards a dozen men, outfit them in the snuggest Levi jeans — a regular Tush-O-Rama — and for the life of me I couldn't tell you which are the hotties and which are the notties. To my eye, all men appear, well, okay. It's not just the posteriors. Be it the torsos, face, legs — it's all the same to me. This is exactly why I am taken aback by Brandt. He's gorgeous, and even I can tell. I'm talking visceral, animal magnetism. Arf.

The specs are easy enough to run through. Stature: quite tall, maybe 6"4'. The eyes: the darkest brown, and shaped like two almonds. Full lips, shining Oxy-white teeth, and a sharp and forceful chin highlight the lower face. Hair: wavy and thick, and though perfectly, and no doubt expensively, cut, gives off that tousled, free-wheeling vibe. Clothes: suede, cotton and showy-unshowy in the manner exclusive to the truly wealthy. Each article of clothing — the chinos, oxford shirt, boat shoes and deep-blue jacket — looks brand-new, clean and glowing. Cat-like is the phrase that captures the lines of his body. Not housecat, not little Tabby, but puma, mountain lion, powerful and sinewy.

The thing is, I could go on dissecting this man down to his cuticles and earlobes, and even if the prose genius of William Faulkner should inhabit my pen, still I could not do justice. It's a case study of the whole being more than the sum of the parts. Let's leave it at this: He exudes it, whatever "it" is.

"Brandt, this was a brilliant idea, just brilliant," Stan says as we head to the hills. "Mixing business and pleasure; you sure know how to play the game. You are the Man, Brandt, no question about it."

It's not just the fawning words, it's the body language, the slightly breathless tone, the entire package. Stan has gotten sycophantism down to an art form. Within the organization that comprises the second largest Ford dealership in Illinois, he has clearly ascended to the coveted position of Toady #1. Among other perquisites, this apparently gets you paid trips to trade shows in appealing locales like Vermont.

"Well, c'mon Stan," the Man replies. "What's the point of coming to Vermont if you don't take a look at the trees?"

Within 20 minutes we have outrun the ever-expanding Burlington urban environs. Once the Holsteins make their appearance, you know you're really in Vermont.

Brandt, meanwhile, is commenting on sundry topics. Stan can barely wait for his boss to get the words out before resoundingly seconding the sentiments. "Brandt, you couldn't be more right. Absolutely!" He's taken the yes-man protocol to new heights. He's the absolutely-man.

At the Cold Hollow cider Mill in Waterbury Center, we pull in to watch the apples get pulverized, and maybe grab a cider donut or two. Waiting on the check-out line, I get a first-hand shot of Brandt's fatal effect on women.

An attractive woman ambles into the store, probably harboring vague thoughts of maple syrup, ceramic mugs and home-made preserves. She passes Brandt, gets — I don't know — a whiff, and stops in her tracks. She stands riveted, drop-jawed as if Martians had zapped her with a ray gun, and just stares at him.

Now it's nothing unusual for people in public spaces to take notice of a sexually attractive stranger. But the notice is taken peripherally, discretely — the looker doesn't want to appear obvious or intrusive to the lookee. Brandt's overwhelming allure short-circuits such social niceties. The woman is out there orbiting planet Hunka-Hunka; all petty earthly concerns have been left far behind. It takes a friend pulling up alongside and literally yanking her by the arm to bring her back to the land of the living. Stepping away, the two of them give each other knowing grins, as the friend mouths the word, "Wow."

Meanwhile Brandt appears oblivious to the ripples of female lust which accompany his movement through the store. The cynosure is where this guy exists, like a light bulb amidst a cluster of moths. I don't think the bulb heeds the moths, either.

Before getting on the highway for the loop back to town, we stop at a nice restaurant in Waterbury. Brandt invites me to join them, which I humbly accept. Who said there's no such thing as a free lunch?

"How are you gentlemen doing today," the waitress greets us, setting down three glasses of water. She's wearing a black miniskirt and a white blouse.

Brandt looks up from the menu, takes in the sight of the attractive questioner, and for the first time, I watch him turn it on.

"Well, honey," he says, "I can't imagine we could possibly be doing any better."

The words are flirty, sure, but nothing special. It's the delivery and the deliveryman that hits the mark. He turns his eyes on this young woman, and it's like the old Superman TV show, when our hero would employ his X-ray vision to see through a wall, and his sight line would be depicted as two, gray expanding cone-shaped fields emanating from his pupils. Our waitress turns into Jell-O encased in a thin layer of skin. For a second, I honestly thought she was going to faint.

"I'll be minute in a back to take your order then," she offers helpfully. Who knew that lust could bring on dyslexia? The three of us watch her turn, lean on an adjoining table, take a deep inhale and wobble back into the kitchen.

Brandt turns to Stan, and with unabashed licentiousness, says, "I bet you she could crack my skull with those thighs." Stan, always the abiding sidekick, replies with the ruttish, "And you'd love it, too."

Brandt takes the napkin from his lap, places it on the table in front of him, rises and says, "Gentlemen, I need to hit the men's room." He's gone not a second when Stan turns to speak with me. I realize this is the first time the two of us are alone on the trip, free to commune peon-to-peon, as it were.

"The guy is disgusting," he whispers, in a hushed urgency. "Not only does he have the looks, but he's fabulously wealthy. He's got a beautiful wife back in Aurora, two of the cutest little kids, and he's boinking women all across the country, from sea to shining sea."

Brandt returns. "All right! Welcome back!" Stan says, his eyes all lit up and shining. His tone expresses ebullience and relief, as if the three-minute separation from his boss was distressing, more than he could reasonably be expected to bear.

I'm dazzled by Stan's head-spinning shift of gears. The guy pivots like a Major League shortstop turning the double play. I feel like I'm at a graduate seminar, "Bootlicking: It's Theory and Practice." Flunkydom, I'm learning, has all the depth of a movie set, the walls of respect and reverence about one inch thick, the mother lode of envy and contempt lurking just below a thin veneer of cleverly fabricated frontage.

The show goes on, the adventures of the sex machine and his faithless servant. Simply another chapter in the Wonderful World of Hacking.

Loving Maria

Regarding personal attire, it takes a startling originality to gain my serious notice. Week in and week out I drive hundreds of people and observe thousands more out on the streets. The visual stimulation is thick, and I've grown a tad jaded. The man — one Trevor McKay — who sat next to me on a trip up to Stowe in early October broke through that fog.

He sported a starched white shirt with a tuxedo ruffle down the front. The shirt was partially covered by a button-down, jet-black vest featuring a raised, gray paisley pattern. A thin, elasticized, black satin band circled his left biceps puckering the shirt fabric — very rakish. His tight black pants had similar black satin strips running down the outer sides, ending at a pair of ornately stitched cowboy boots. Upon his head roosted an over-sized black Stetson with two gray feathers dangling from a leather cord off the rear. In his right earlobe — what else? — a black pearl. What made the ensemble yet more eye-catching was the stature of the clotheshorse himself. The man stood five feet tall, if that. The overall effect was something like the Lollipop Guild of Munchkinland gone urban cowboy. Yee-haw!

"You understand that the Trapp Family Lodge is my interest," he said. Trevor's voice rose high-pitched and nasal — uncannily like the late Truman Capote. "I know we spoke of a tour, but it's really the Lodge I want to visit."

"It's your day, my friend," I assured my skittish customer. "We'll head right up there and spend as much time as you want."

I glanced over to my right and saw Trevor give a wide smile, relaxing into his seat.

"The day is gorgeous," I continued, "the trees are going off with all kinds of color; you couldn't have picked a better time for the visit. If you don't mind me asking, why the Trapp Family Lodge?"

"Oh God, where to begin?" I could hear the thrill in his voice." My mom was mad for musical theater. We lived in New Haven, and we would get the Broadway plays during their out-of-town tryouts. Well, it must have been 1957 or eight — I was all of 13 years-old — when she took me to see *The Sound of Music*. I was enthralled, simply enchanted. The triumph, against all odds, of this glorious young woman filled my soul. Wouldn't you know that mom took me backstage. God knows how she pulled that one off!" I could see his eyes were in a twinkling reverie.

"Anyway, I met Mary Martin. You know, she played Maria Von Trapp on the stage. In the movie, of course, it was Julie Andrews — who also did a marvelous job, by the way. Miss Martin could not have been more lovely to me. What a classy lady!"

"So it all goes back to the late '50's in Connecticut, huh?" I injected.

"Heavens no! That was merely the beginning. Of course, I bought the cast album when it became available, and memorized all the songs. Then in '63 my mom and I left one late Friday night to journey up to Stowe. We were supposed to leave the Saturday morning, but neither of us could sleep, what with all the excitement."

"Was the Lodge already in operation back then?" I asked.

"Oh yes. It started as a music school of sorts, you know. Maria would teach singing. But, by popular demand, really, it had evolved into a hotel by the early '60's."

"So, didja get to meet Maria?"

"Did I ever! She spoke warmly with me and mom a few times during the weekend visit. She carried herself with an almost regal aloofness, some would say, but we got to know the real Maria, a woman of compassion and true generosity."

We were speeding through the Bolton Flats, that incongruous table of level land nestled amidst the surrounding hillsides. It is upon this long, flat straight-away that the Burlington Airport cabs rendezvous with the inspectors to get their taxi meters tested and certified. The maple trees along this stretch were in full dress color, the fulfillment of every leaf peeper's desire. My tourist, however, only had eyes for Maria's place, and thus remained within his own thoughts as we drove on.

Arriving at the Lodge, Trevor suggested lunch at the Austrian Tea Room. We negotiated our way through the menu which features 20 varieties of Wiener schnitzel, and we appreciated our helpful, dirndl-attired waitress. It was then off to the main lodge. Trevor knew exactly what he wanted to see having made this pilgrimage quite a few times. The hallowed grounds were his Graceland, the departed matriarch his Elvis.

In the early '80's, the original main lodge was completely destroyed in a devastating fire. Someone — I remember reading the newspaper accounts at the time but can't recall whether it was a guest or a hotel work-er — perished in the blaze. The rebuilt lodge is enormous, magnificent and unabashedly alpine. Curlicue, Christmas tree-shaped peaks everywhere adorn the massive exterior. I noticed a wide stone path which appeared to curve up into a grassy courtyard adjoining the building, and I asked Trevor about it.

"These were the steps to the old lodge," he said, and he led the way up. On the green expanse was a small enclosed graveyard, the final resting place of a number of family members, including Maria herself. Beside the tiny cemetery stood a lonesome, gnarled and weather-beaten tree, which we approached.

"Do you see these notches on the trunk?" he asked. "They're from the fire. This old tree is all that remains." He slowly raised his arm and softly placed four fingers on the fire scars. A few shiny tears slid down his cheek as he bowed and shook his head. "Okay — enough of this!" he suddenly barked. "No use dwelling in the past. Let's explore the new lodge."

The lobby was well-populated, this being the heart of the foliage sea-son, but the front desk manager spotted Trevor amidst the hubbub.

"Mr. McKay, what a pleasure," he said, walking up to us and extend-ing a hand to Trevor. "We didn't expect you again this season. To what do we owe this honor?"

"John, you are a darling," Trevor said, clearly relishing the special attention. "I was visiting the family in Connecticut and simply could not resist another visit. It's so stunning this time of year."

"Well, enjoy yourself," said the manager. "Roam about to your heart's content!"

I shadowed Trevor as he traipsed through the four floors and many wings of the big building. The hotel is still run by the Von Trapp family and the loving attention to detail was abundant. Every section was spark-ing clean, handsomely appointed. Around every corner, sitting rooms abounded with sumptuously upholstered couches and companion easy chairs. Everywhere the walls were covered with Von Trapp memorabilia, including priceless oriental rugs the family managed to secrete out of Europe as they fled the Nazis. There were endless old photographs of their idyllic pre-war life, including line-ups of robust, red-cheeked smiling children.

On the top floor, Trevor searched out a particular alcove. Tucked on a back wall near the door of a utility closet, he found what he was looking for and called me over.

"Look at this," he said, his right hand resting on his heart. "Isn't this too much?"

I bent forward to look at a framed eight-by-ten of Mary Martin on stage in full wedding dress for the scene of Maria's marriage to Baron Von Trapp. On the bottom was written: "To my dearest Maria, The joy of my life has been playing you, knowing you, and Loving You. (signed) Mary Martin." The words, "Loving You", were twice the size of the others.

Was it too much? How easy to scoff at this curious lifelong devotion to the grande dame, the play, the lodge, the mythology. Yes, I started the trip with an unvoiced derision toward Trevor, but by the end I had dropped all judgment. There's a human urge, maybe even imperative, to believe in something or someone larger than oneself. Certainly this delightful diminutive man could have done a lot worse than to apotheosize the genuinely inspiring figure of Baroness Maria Von Trapp.

Hackie 2000

The first widespread snowstorm coated northern Vermont in mid-December. The evening news broadcast the inevitable film of vehicles spun off the highway, beaming skiers and snowboarders and the sober warning from the state transportation spokesperson to stay off the roads unless "absolutely necessary".

Everywhere there was significant accumulation, as high as a foot and a half in Stowe. Burlington — and only Burlington — had zero, I mean barely a trace. It was the oddest snowfall pattern I had seen in my 20-plus years in the north country. Driving my taxi on a Saturday night, the streets were perfectly dry. Every so often, I'd notice a passing car — obviously from out of the area — its bumper and top piled with fresh snow, its side panels streaked with slush, salt and road gravel.

I was grateful Burlington had somehow dodged the storm. While severe snow conditions increase the number of calls, you can't make any time — as anyone who has driven during and in the aftermath of a blizzard knows all too well. For cabbies, this translates into fewer fares per hour, and less revenue. In any case, I'm too old for vigilant, white-knuckled driving — when the white stuff seriously flies, I put out the "closed" sign and pack it in.

It had been a decent Saturday night for the time of year. Most students were studying for finals or had finished up and gone home for the semester break. The locals don't go out much in December; free time is filled with shopping and preparation for the holiday festivities. Tourism and business conferences are likewise on hold during the lead-up to Christmas. As the night wound down, I was glad to have a few bucks in my shirt pocket. On a last spin through downtown, a thirtyish man hailed me with a waving left hand; in his right hand he held a bulging gyro sandwich. As I pulled to meet him at the curb, he attacked his hand-food with a lusty chomp while he opened the front door to speak to me.

"You want to take me to Richmond?" he asked in garbled gyro-speak.

"I don't see why the heck not," I said, and off we took.

As we headed south on 89, it was like entering another climactic zone. Passing through Williston, snow started appearing on the sides of the road; by Richmond, the snow was falling quietly, with steady force. My escape from the storm had lasted up until the last run of the night.

He had me pull into a driveway next to a general store in downtown Richmond. "This is my place," he said. "I just gotta run in to pick up something and I'll be right out." I sat in the taxi watching the snowflakes land and evaporate on the windshield, and in less than five minutes, he returned with a bag in his arm filled with grocery items.

"Listen," he said, "my car's right here, but I'm really in no shape to drive. Could you take me up to Bolton Valley? I live in one of the condos up there. I'll pay you whatever you need."

Though the ski area is called "Bolton Valley", it's anything but. It's a mountain, with a bear of an access road, the bane of Burlington cabbies. On a snowy night like this, I knew it would be straining the transmission on the way up, and hell on the brakes on the way down. But this is my job; the guy was being responsible by not driving after drinking; I wasn't going to abandon him in Richmond.

I said, "That's going to be a hectic trip on a night like this, you know. If you hadn't noticed, this ride ain't exactly an SUV. I'll take you, but I gotta get 60 bucks."

"How about I give you $100? I appreciate what you're doing."

Whoa! I thought — that's what I call serious appreciation. "Well, the $60 will be fine," I said, "but I won't turn down a good tip. Let's get you up there."

Through Jonesville and into the town of Bolton, snow was everywhere — on the ground, in the air — and the road was greasy, as the Vermonters say. The first-of-the-season confrontation with winter conditions is always stressful, especially so since the near absence of snow in Burlington had lulled me into complacency, if not denial. But I quickly adjusted. It's all so familiar — the frigid air, the gleaming white; the foggy, frosted windows; the steady crunch under the wheels.

We swung a left onto the access road and began the long ascent to the ski area. From years of experience, I know that low gear, slow and steady, gets the job done on these mountain inclines, and steadily we climbed.

"Man, there's a ton of snow up here," I said to my customer. "It's great that the ski area finally has the solid ownership to get this place happening again. I've heard this mountain has some fabulous skiing."

"You got that right," he replied. "This area is a for-real snow belt. It's always snowing up here. I've seen days when Sugarbush or Stowe gets nada, and we're buried."

The higher we rose, the more beautiful it became. The headlights illuminated the dark woods etched in glistening ice and snow. It was all mysteriously enchanting, the way Vermont gets, the way we love it. There was no more talking now, and the silence was natural, and it was peaceful — just me in the front, my customer in the back and the gently swirling snow whooshing against the vehicle as we moved through space. The driving settled into a comfortable groove; I took a deep breath, and my thoughts drifted.

I thought of the two thousand year mark, just days away. Whether or not this benchmark in time carries an intrinsic meaning is beyond my understanding, yet I clearly sensed some power of the date washing over me and filling me with reflection. I gazed out into the twinkling night air and felt a wave of deep feeling. I couldn't tell if it was sadness or joy; it seemed to spring from a place in my heart deeper, more fundamental than pure emotion. What felt like ancient tears rose to my eyes. I found myself silently mouthing the words, "Thank you", though I'm not sure to whom it was directed.

In that instant this thought came to me: I don't know to where our souls journey when we die, but I hope the place feels something like this mountain, at this moment.

5

The Taxi Trade

*As in any profession, the taxi business has its inside skinny —
the news and information kept within the brotherhood.
Well, I'm blabbing, breaking the silence.*

Why I Ran Over Crazy Walter

Jim, the Amtrak stationmaster, is looking at me with a scrunched up, quizzical expression. We go back 20 years, so I know a question is coming.

"Jernigan," he says, "one of the other cabbies was talking about you, and he mentioned something that sounded off-the-wall. Still, I have to ask you. Did you run over a fellow cabbie a few years back?"

"Pshaw!" I say. "Jim, does that sound like me? Really, now. You know how these cabbies are. Rumors upon rumors."

Then, as I pause, the whole incident comes rushing back to me.

"Actually, Jim, now that you mention it, I did run over another cabbie once. It happened right out here, as a matter of fact."

Jim is now looking at me with his mouth slightly open, eyebrows raised.

"You want to hear about it, I suppose."

"What do you think?" Jim answers with a smile.

"Well, it's a long story," I say.

"All the better; the train's late tonight."

Here we go again, I thought, as the bus pulled into the terminal. I was sitting in my taxi, parked in the first-out position of the taxi queue. Crazy Walter sat in the two-spot, sipping his omni-present liter of Mountain Dew. I read that Mountain Dew contains something like triple the caffeine of black coffee. That being the case, anyone even vaguely familiar with Crazy Walter would tell you this is the last thing he should be ingesting on a regular basis.

The bus discharged its passengers; a couple approached my cab. The rule at the bus terminal is simple: no soliciting. You sit in your vehicle until the customer comes to you. In a flash, Walter was out of his car, grabbing the people's luggage, hustling them towards his taxi. So now I was out of my taxi, eye-to-eye with him. I believe in non-violence, but I can't let the other drivers intimidate me if I expect to make a living out in these streets.

"For Chrissakes, Walter, let's not go through this again," I said as calmly as I could muster. This was far from my first go around with this guy. "You know this is my fare."

"What you talkin' about! This is my fare!" Walter was flailing his arms as he screamed at me, no easy task with a bag in each hand. "You always trying to take all the work!"

Meanwhile the couple was standing by Walter's cab, a look of minor alarm on their faces. I detest playing out these hackie squabbles in front of customers; to me it looks so, well, unprofessional.

Walter pushed passed me and threw the bags into his trunk. "Get in! Get in!" he yelled at the now cowering couple. He then jumped into his seat, slammed the door, and sped away.

What term is in vogue now? Emotionally imbalanced? Bi-polar? Karmically challenged? How about this one: the guy was nuts. Hence the nickname. Cabbies, as you may have guessed, don't go in much for political correctness. There was a cabbie many years back who had lost his right arm up to his elbow in a farming accident when he was a kid. All the guys called him, "One-arm". And that's when they were being nice. Otherwise they called him, "Flipper".

Walter was a refugee from one of those Balkan countries, Slovakia, Slovenia — I never could get the story straight. Don't ask me why he took up cabdriving. I suppose hacking has always been a classic job for the new immigrant. He arrived in town around the time of the first Gulf War, and I guess for this reason, his other nickname was, "The Iranian". *Close enough* was the prevailing attitude.

From the beginning, his behavior around the other drivers was erratic. Before long, we cabbies began to trade Crazy Walter stories, as in, "Jeezum, you won't believe what the Iranian pulled last night . . ."

Which brings us, at some later date, out to the Amtrak station in Essex Junction. Before meeting the incoming evening train, I've learned to call ahead. On occasion it's late, so checking arrivals in advance avoids dead time. On this particular night, my timing was right on the money; as I passed the fairgrounds on Route 15, I could hear the train whistle out by IBM, a mile or so away. Approaching the station, I saw the red crossing-signal lights were already blinking, the bell clanging. I also observed Crazy Walter standing beside his taxi, glaring at me.

There was but one available parking position, right next to Walter's cab. As I made the wide turn to slide in, Walter scooted into the spot and faced me, arms extended in front of him, hands up. Apparently, he had decided I wasn't to park there. Even by his own aberrant standards, this was fairly bizarre conduct.

Unfortunately for Walter, I had not had a good day. Or maybe it was the years of bedeviling provocations come to its natural breaking point. In any event, I advanced at 5 m.p.h. directly toward him. He grinned at me like Rasputin, his eyes afire. The warning lights were flashing, the bells sounding, the train whistle shrieking.

The odd thing is, I never considered *not* running him down. I can't for the life of me — now reviewing my actions — ever recall weighing the decision: should, or should I not, run Walter over?

Our eyes locked. It was a game of chicken that he lost purely by weight. He never flinched until the bumper hit his thighs. He was upended onto the front hood, then slid off the vehicle to the right — splat onto the pavement.

I'm not proud of my behavior. For one thing, you don't have to be the Dalai Lama to recognize it as something other than non-violence. And we all know what violence begets.

Walter jumped up in a flash. Thankfully, owing to my slow rate of speed, he didn't appear to be seriously hurt. "You frickin' crazy Pontiac, I kill you!" he bellowed, as he commenced pounding on my driver's window with clenched fist. At that moment, I came to my senses, backed up and vamoosed. I later discovered that he had lodged a criminal complaint against me with the Essex Police Department, but due to, I suppose, his reputation and demeanor, they never even contacted me about it.

"Well, Jernigan, you never cease to amaze me." Jim says. "That is the damnedest cabbie story I've ever heard."

"That may be," I respond, "but it still leaves one obvious question unanswered."

"And what's that?" Jim says.

"Which of us crazy hackies is more nuts: Walter — or me?"

Big Phil's Gone

It's funny how time works its sleight of hand. For the longest time I was one of the young guys, and then — poof! — I'm one of the old guys. For the life of me, I can't recall the transition, the moment of metamorphosis; it's like it happened in my sleep.

There's but a handful of cabbies around from the early days, just a few of us who have witnessed the transformation of Burlington from the still sleepy, glorified small town of the '70s, to the bustling, relatively cosmopolitan city of the new millennium. There's an unspoken bond among us old guys, a knowing look as our taxis cross on the street and we nod or raise a couple of fingers in greeting.

Big Phil was one of the old-timers, a hackie "lifer" who drove for one of the big fleets. Unlike many of us, he never made the move over to self-employment as an independent owner-operator. Driving for the fleets is tough, grinding work; though an experienced driver can make decent money — by working stiff standards, anyway — every last penny is earned. The 12-hour shifts are exhausting, and the job lacks the most basic fringe benefits that even a tyro burger-flipper can expect these days.

In my experience, the long-term fleet drivers fall into two categories: those with great self-esteem, a robust sense of self, and those with horrendous self-esteem, essentially doormats walking. The former have a way of laughing off the shoddy treatment dished out by the fleet owners — and their lieutenants, the dispatchers — and sticking up for themselves when it really matters. The latter are subject to increasingly demeaning treatment as time goes by, until these poor guys are ultimately reduced to a serf-like servility.

It's painful to witness, and Big Phil — a loud, big-hearted, Kodiak of a man — was sadly and firmly under the thumb of his boss.

On and off through the years — in discussions at the taxi stands, the bus depot, the train station — I encouraged him to go independent. "After all," I'd say, "you know the streets as well as anyone, you know all the tricks of the trade. Jeezum, Philly, why the heck not?"

He'd reply, "Jernigan, you're absolutely right. I'm gonna save up the money for a decent vehicle and the insurance down-payment, and I'm gonna do it!"

Sometimes we'd even discuss the pros and cons of various model cars as worthy taxis; sometimes he would go so far as to ask for the phone number of a taxi supply company that sells taxi lights. "A big green one," he'd say. "I honestly think the big colored lights attract more customers."

But it never went beyond the talk. Truth is, the whole thing was *my* idea, not his. Like some low-rent Tony Robbins, I'd enlist him in my enthusiasm, and he'd run with it — more to please me, I expect, than out of any strong desire on his part.

Eventually I came to my senses and dropped the gratuitous exhortation. Independent hacking is no bed of roses, and beyond that, it occurred to me that Big Phil might actually know what's best for Big Phil — a revolutionary notion in my egocentric universe.

Picturing Big Phil in my mind's eye, I find myself thinking about summer, because, whereas winter keeps us cabbies encased in our heated vehicles, the summer heat eggs us out to stretch, mingle and schmooze. (Cabbies, in case you haven't caught on, live to talk, talk, talk.)

A bunch of us are lined up at the Main Street taxi stand, it could be the early '90s, maybe it's a hazy July night. The noise, the lights, the dewy air — it's summertime in Vermont's big town. Things are slow for the time being and we don't mind, because tonight, for some reason, it feels right to linger and confabulate.

With his tremendous girth, Big Phil is spending maximum time outside of his vehicle. For him, the summer cab is truly a sweatbox — even when he's lucky enough to get one of the rare fleet cabs with a functioning air-conditioner. We stand side-by-side leaning against the driver side of his cab. Every couple of minutes he does his elaborate back-scratching routine against the door handle, looking like some impossibly overfed two-legged cat. There's a grace to his movements, an unexpected delicacy.

We're vaguely watching the raucous teenagers who drive by, their sound systems booming the bass so beyond-loud, the reverberation so unearthly, I feel like my internal organs are about to pulverize. A lot of the kids know Big Phil; he's been a presence out here in the public arena for a long time. They know his susceptibility to taunts, and the more ill-natured of them hurl insults trying to get him going. Every so often he obliges, and shouting matches that result are a sight to behold.

Years earlier I'd given up suggesting other "options" for dealing with these whippersnappers. I'd discovered that unqualified acceptance of Big Phil's many eccentricities made for a better relationship.

This summer, Big Phil won't be around; he's moved to — of all places — Florida. Since his departure, I find myself trying to visualize "Big Phil in the Sunshine State". I see him behind the wheel of a candy-orange taxi driving down palm-lined streets. His fares are — I don't know — retirees, drug-dealers, alligators, Mickey Mice? The picture never quite gels.

Big Phil belongs back here in the Queen City. The thing is, I miss him.

The Muffin Report

Late June, and it was pouring. Again. What was it, the 20th straight day? Since when did we switch climates with Bangladesh? It was the start of my workday and I was feeling ornery.

A dose of current events was only likely to exacerbate my foul mood, so don't ask me to explain the perverse impulse which found me looking for a store that sold newspapers. As I pulled into the parking area fronting the Cheese Outlet, the rain — against all odds — kicked into yet a higher gear of true monsoon dimensions. To avoid a total drenching, I stopped direct-ly in front of the short stairs to the entrance. Though this position blocked in some other vehicles, I knew I'd be in and out in less than 30 seconds. I dashed up the three stairs and paused for a moment under the awning's pro-tection. A middle-aged man stood there munching on a muffin.

"How the hell do you think people are supposed to get out?" he asked in a chiding tone.

I ignored him, scooted inside and bought the paper. Now 30 seconds later, I was under the canopy, again standing beside the Muffin Man. I was gathering myself momentarily for the 10-foot sprint to the taxi. Somebody once said if you move quickly enough, you can dodge the raindrops. I was readying myself to test that hypothesis.

"What the hell's a matter with you?" he screamed at me, picking up where he left off moments ago. "Move that goddam taxi!"

Now I had two voices speaking in my head at approximately equal resonance. In my left ear, I heard, "You don't have to take this abuse! Stick it back at 'em — he deserves it." In my right ear, I heard, "Let it go, Jernigan. This has nothing to do with you. The guy's probably having a rough day."

I chose to follow the voice in the left ear. I moved towards the guy, positioning my face six inches from his. I then said calmly, evenly, very softly, "Eat shit."

Sparks flew from his head and torso. It was an electrifying moment.

"That's it, jerk," he said. "You've had it!"

In disbelief, I watched transfixed as he went tearing into the rain to his car, and grabbed a pen and pad from the dashboard. Dripping with rain, he then charged up to my vehicle and furiously copied my license number. A half-eaten muffin lay at my feet. I gazed down at it and felt a strange sadness, as if it was a little birdie fallen from the safety of its nest. I jumped into the taxi and vamoosed.

Two minutes up the road, I spun around and returned to the scene of the crime. My intention was to apologize. Regardless of the man's actions, my words were completely uncalled for. Actually, they were called for, as I said, by the voice in my left ear. But that's not my code of conduct, doing what the voices in my head tell me to do. Alas, when I pulled back into the lot, he was gone. A gut feeling, however, told me this isn't the last of this incident.

I love City Hall. Despite the interior modernization it's undergone, it still retains a lot of old-fashioned flourishes such as the Full Monty urinals, the kind with the bowls at floor level, one of which I now stand before.

I am at City Hall enjoying a delightful antediluvian urination, because the Muffin Man has taken the time to fax a letter to the Honorable Mayor Peter Clavelle reporting my dastardly behavior that fateful day at the Cheese Outlet, and ending with, "I ask the City to take this incident seriously when this operator's license comes up for renewal."

Well, take it seriously they did, because the License Committee sent me a letter "requesting my attendance" on this matter. I had this minor incentive to honor this request: All City taxi licenses are renewed in July, and my application was being held up pending the result of this meeting.

Now it's three o'clock, and I'm sitting in Conference Room #1 with a dozen other people. From the conversations going on around me, I surmise that most of them are here on liquor and tobacco license appeals. Yup, I'm the sole reprobate cabbie in the room.

In come the Commissioners, two clean-cut thirty-something guys. It's pretty laid back. Nobody announces, "All rise" or anything like that. They just waltz in, wearing street clothes, sit down at the table in the middle of the room, and one of them asks the secretary what's first up. I pipe up at this point, asking if they could deal with my matter first because I'm working today (as if all these other people weren't). They glance at each other, one says, "Sure", and they commence to reading the Muffin Report. Each one has a copy. They finish at the same time, look at each other again, and one says to me, "Well, what do you say about this?"

Given the opportunity, I am prolix to the point of inducing physical pain on the part of the listener. Truly, the sound of my own voice is the sweetest music to my ears. I begin my response at the point of my driver's test at age 16. Finally, after what is near *War and Peace* duration, I end with this nifty envoi: "This action is not my style. The disputed details are unimportant to me. (In his *J'accuse* letter, the guy had claimed that he had told me to move because he himself was waiting in his car to get out.) I feel bad about what I did. If you think it would settle this matter, I'd like to send the guy an apology letter, and copy the Licensing Committee."

The Licensing Committee, all two of them, look at each other — I'm beginning to think they have some telepathic thing going — nod at me in tandem, and one says, "Yeah, that'll work for us."

There's a lesson to be learned from this near debacle, and believe you me, it has not been lost on your savvy cabbie. When it's raining, I never, *ever* go to the Cheese Outlet.

5: THE TAXI TRADE

Quid Pro Quo

"Hey, would ya please? This itch is drivin' me nuts. Whaddaya mean, 'What's in it for me?' I'll tell ya what: you scratch my back and I'll scratch yours."

Is this not what human intercourse, of every variety, boils down to?

Every cabbie has something of value, a non-material asset, yet one to which it is possible to assign a price. This nebulous commodity is a recommendation. Countless times a week, cabbies get these inquiries: "What's a good place to eat in this town?" In lieu of "eat" you can fill in "rent a car", "stay for the night", or "have a drink". And by and large, the customer takes the cabbie's suggestion. Naive simpleton that I am, it took me quite a while to recognize the possibilities.

One summer evening, early in the eighties, I picked up two French-Canadian couples who had arrived in town via a large, sumptuously-appointed sailing vessel. They immediately asked the best place for an Italian meal. I responded with a short description of the one or two Italian eateries that existed back then. The next question was about the wine lists, and from that I deduced they desired a truly classy place. I mentioned a renowned five-star establishment just north of Waterbury Center, adding that I'd be more than glad to transport them round-trip, helpful guy that I am. "Why not? Let's go," was the response. Obviously, these folks had bucks. Aside from the taxi fare, the meal at this joint with wine, tax and tip could easily run $250 for the foursome.

We arrived at Trattoria Mucho Deluxo, and I waited in the vehicle while my customers entered to dine. I figured I'd attack the Times crossword puzzle while they ate. However, within five minutes a small man, nattily attired in an impeccable black suit, white boutonniere and rosy tie, came out to my taxi.

"My friend, come inside to my restaurant," he said. "I'm going to feed you."

Apparently, my customers had told him that they were there on my recommendation. He led me through a rear entrance and sat me down at a small table located in an alcove off the kitchen. He then spoke to the cook, who was decked out in full battle gear, including the cool white cylinder hat, which in the moment struck me as a miniature of the Leaning Tower of Pisa.

"Paulo, you give our friend here anything he wants. He's our special guest. No vino, though." He glanced at me and winked. "He's driving tonight."

I chatted a little with Paulo, made my choice, and soon was present-ed with a pastel-colored porcelain plate, the size of a hubcap, piled high with some divine version of Pasta Alfredo. Understand that my mother, God love her, was a remarkably inept cook. An "Italian" dinner in my home was overcooked Ronzoni splattered with catsup and melted Velveeta "cheese". The dish that then sat in front of me related gustatorially to my Mom's recipe in the manner that Shakespeare's *A Midsummer Night's Dream* relates dramatically to an average episode of "Baywatch". The smell alone made me weep tears of joy. I ate. It was the best meal of my life.

As I left with my customers, the owner discretely pulled me aside and drove the point home. "Anytime you bring tourists to me like tonight," he said, "you can count on another meal." Point taken!

Though this delicious experience opened my eyes, I never pursued the possibilities as the months and years passed. That is, until recently.

A couple months ago, it occurred to me that I've been suggesting a newly-refurbished local Bed & Breakfast to a number of visitors, and tak-ing them there for overnight bookings and longer. I've recommended the place because it's close to downtown and it seems like a great place to stay in contrast to a look-alike hotel room. Then a light bulb appeared over my head, and in that light bulb these words appeared: "Remember the Pasta!"

The next day I put on a nice shirt, headed over to the B & B, and made a proposal to the quite aristocratic owner. "Your least expensive rooms are close to $100. I'll funnel tourists to your place at $10 a pop. Do we got a deal?"

She got this look on her face that reminded me of the expression my dachshund would get when he mistakenly gobbled up some particularly distasteful spillage off the city street. My jarring lack of discretion was the problem.

"Are you talking about — and here she paused for a moment, dropped her eyes, and whispered conspiratorially, as if the FTC might have posted listening devices for just this eventuality — a kickback?"

I felt like shooting back, "Your darn tootin', Honey!", but by this point I have taken at least a basic reading of the person with whom I was dealing, and I modulated my response accordingly.

"Well, I don't think we need to call it that. It's more like a 'referral fee', like you might pay to a travel agent who books a client at your place." I somehow manage to refrain from adding, "After all, 'kickback' is such an ugly word."

She agreed, and over the course of the next few weeks I did bring her a few guests. I then asked around and discovered that travel agents and tour guides regularly receive 20-25% for referrals of this kind, and I brought this information to the B & B lady, informing her that I'd like to raise my kickback, excuse me, referral fee to $20. Greed had grabbed me by the wallet. She said absolutely not, there was sort of an argument, and that was the end of that relationship.

I'm glad. I felt lousy every time I had brought somebody there knowing I had a financial stake. I get paid for driving people. Suggesting shops, restaurants, hotels and places to see is a great joy for me. I love our city and derive pleasure in sharing my insider knowledge. Getting paid for it was like ladling Velveeta on the Pasta Alfredo.

When I received that great Italian meal years ago, it had occurred naturally, with no calculation on my part. That was delicious. Kickbacks, it seems, taste sour to me.

Honest

There's a guy I often drive home from a downtown club. It's a notable fare because it's highly unusual for someone in his sixties to spend late nights at a bar populated by the usual twenty-somethings. The man lives in one of Burlington's old-age apartment developments. Although the term is properly applied only by self-definition, this person is clearly alcoholic. He's friendly enough though, and the bouncer always seems genuinely happy to help the guy safely into my taxi. From nights when he's capable of snippets of coherent conversation, I've gleaned that he's a lifetime local. Like that favorite Vermont joke: Q. Have you lived here your whole life? A. Not yet.

When he pays the fare, he's completely careless with his money. A crumpled-up thicket of small and large bills emerges in a calloused fist, generally after a haphazard reconnoiter through any number of pants, coat and shirt pockets. There's every possibility of dropped money. Which brings up a question that keeps coming back to me: Is honesty its own reward?

When I was a kid driving a yellow checker taxi in New York City, I once drove a gentleman from midtown to his Park Avenue apartment. I doubt there are two dozen houses in the entire state of Vermont with the valuation of an average pre-WW II Park Avenue apartment house. These properties never change hands for less than a million dollars. The point is, anyone living in this locale is extremely wealthy.

The meter read a few dollars, and he placed some bills into the small pass-through compartment. In New York City taxis, the customer and driver are separated by a Plexiglas partition between the front and rear seats. This device thwarts the temptation to punch, stab and shoot each another. When I removed the bills to count, I saw that he had inadvertently given me three singles and a twenty instead of four singles. In the mid-

'70's, a twenty was a twenty; my net for a good shift — commission plus tips — was only about 40 dollars. The guy then asked, "Did I just give you four singles?"

If I hesitated a millisecond, I don't think he noticed. "Yes, you sure did, sir," I replied, as I passed him back eighty cents change. He looked at me askance — I couldn't look him in the eyes, but caught his demeanor peripherally — and dropped a thirty-five cent tip into the cup as he exited.

Here's the thought process of that 20 year-old cabdriver. Mao Tsetung wrote that political power comes out of a barrel of a gun. It hasn't come to that here, yet. In the meantime, it's perfectly legitimate to partake in a little wealth redistribution if it falls into my lap. Plus, I really *need* the money (to each according to his need), while 20 bucks means nothing to this blueblood guy. For the next hour after this fare, I diverted the twinges of guilt by elaborately calculating whether 20 dollars for the Park Avenue man was equivalent to one, five or 10 cents to me. I think I finally decided on a nickel.

Move the cursor to "Greed" and click. Now scan down to "Rationalization" and click again. Hey, that's not a bad picture of me.

I'd like to believe I've come along in my ethical understanding in two decades. Present-day me now gives Park Avenue guy back the money. But sometimes the territory is not so clear-cut, and finding my moral bearings is a real challenge.

Last week, as a fairly obnoxious customer left the vehicle, I noticed a ten on the floor of the rear seat where he had been sitting. Was it his? I knew if I asked he would claim it in a flash, regardless of the truth. On the other hand, there was a strong possibility it *was* his 10 dollars. I called to him on the sidewalk, "Hey, any chance you dropped 10 bucks while you were paying me?"

He took out his wallet and looked — made a show of looking? — into it. "As a matter of fact, I did," he replied, and walked to my window, took the ten without a word of thanks, and turned and walked back to his house. It's at moments like this I wonder — what kind of fool am I?

Another scenario is the over-generous drunk. Do you accept an absurdly large tip from a customer who clearly can't afford it, but in a besotted haze, has decided you're his bestest friend in the whole world? Generally, I'll ask if he knows how much he's given me, and does he really want to do it. If he then insists I take it, I will. There's something to the old proverbs. For instance, if someone presents you with a horse, just take it. Do not pause to pull apart the horse's lips, pry open the teeth, and look inside.

Which brings us back to our old, intoxicated local. The last time I drove him, I noticed $45 in his seat just after he left. In this situation, I knew it was his money. I ran into the lobby and caught him waiting for the elevator.

"You dropped this money," I said and handed him the $45. He looked at me uncomprehendingly, reached out, took the cash and stuck it in his pocket. His failure to thank me did not reflect ingratitude; he simply was too drunk to grasp what happened and respond appropriately.

I did the right thing, huh? Outwardly, yes. But check out the interior monologue. When I returned the money and the old guy neglected to thank me for this noble act of honesty (*so* beyond the call of duty, *so* much more than expected from your average cabdriver), I was fuming the rest of the night.

"If that's his attitude, I was an idiot for giving the money back to him". Such was my thought process, as if an act of integrity is contingent on a desired response. It's not enough to be honest; I need to be *acknowledged* for being honest.

Who needs self-improvement seminars? My job generates all the lessons I can handle.

5: THE TAXI TRADE

To Burp, Perchance to Heave

Hackie is a book about cabdriving. As such, there is a subject that can no longer be avoided; it must be broached. It is not a pleasant subject and I've put it off as long as possible. Further delay would be a breach of my professional duty. For the faint of heart, or more to the point, weak of stomach, now is your chance to bail out. There will be no further warnings.

In order, these are the three worst things to a cabdriver: an accident, a robbery, vomit. The first two are self-explanatory; let's talk about the third.

"Granted", you might observe, "a customer throwing up in your taxi is certainly unpleasant, but is it so odious as to rank third on the "Pantheon of Hackie Horribles"?

The immediate response is that unpleasant does not do justice to the specter of a vomit-sprayed cab interior. Once the customer blows, you're toast — your night is over. You can't go, "Oh tish-tish, what a mess. I'll have to clean it up at the end of the night." No, the reality is: go directly to the car wash, do not pass "go", do not collect $200. The cleaning process is measured in hours not minutes, and by night's end, you're left with soaking seats and that inimitable lingering odor.

In the face of such dire consequences, cabbies become hyper-vigilant in discerning the warning signals. In 90% of the cases, the potential puker is thoroughly intoxicated, so you can't rely on the normal process of self-regulation. Constant small burping noises are a very bad sign, the equivalent of those ominous gas emissions preceding a volcanic eruption. Proclamations such as, "I'm not feeling very good", go unheeded at your own peril.

I've learned the hard way to take immediate prophylactic action. I look the pre-regurgitator right in the eyes and say loudly and clearly, "If you feel, even vaguely, like you have to throw up, tell me right away so I can stop the cab and let you out. I don't mind false alarms; let's be safe rather than sorry."

This simple warning has served me well: I've succeeded in reducing the daily odds to about 1 in 365. Once a month a customer does his or her thing by the side of the road, but remarkably, I have gone a full year without an in-cab deposit. Recently, however, the string was broken.

Last week, when a customer picked my taxi as the ideal site for an explosion of projectile vomiting — well, I was bummed but philosophical. As the bumper sticker says, "Shit Happens", and once a year is bearable. Wisk, ammonia, sponges, vacuum, brushes and plenty of water seemed to do the trick. The following morning I purchased six green, Christmas tree-shaped, car fresheners — "Royal Pine" scent — and hung them strategically throughout the vehicle. End of incident — good riddance.

Later that evening, on the lovely Circumferential Highway *en route* to Essex Center, a 240-pound partied-out rugby player gave me the redux treatment of the previous night. The only substantive difference was, this second night, the volume was greater.

I turned to tear into the offender, but this great bear of a guy was already slobberly apologizing all over the place. He handed me $20, which I took, and offered to help with the cleanup, which I declined. Maybe his drunkenness heightened the emotional tenor, but the entire turn of events was clearly affecting him.

He actually looked as if he was about to start crying. This was in sharp contrast to the previous night's perpetrator who was pie-eyed beyond all meaningful awareness of his actions. Although last-night's guy truly deserved it, yelling at him would have yielded all the satisfaction of reprimanding a flounder.

As we pulled up to his place, the guy had a look of pure despondency. Momentarily transcending my freaked-out state — two nights in a row of these festivities had left me somewhat, well, "unhinged" — I told him, "Buddy, you have handled this bad situation with as much class as is humanly possible."

With that, he visibly brightened and wobbled down the driveway and stepped into his house. Hooray for him.

Ah, Lady Luck, my fickle mistress. In high school I barely passed the math classes but, if memory serves me, the odds of consecutive night fulminations are 1 in 365 squared! Let's round it out to 1 in 100,000.

Gadzooks! I think that qualifies as astronomically. Have I not paid sufficient tribute to the Taxi Gods?

The previous month I had caught a fare to Burlington, Ontario. Was that not incredibly lucky? Were my twin nights of vomit some manner of payback, all part of the cosmic balancing act? Such was my thought process that second night at the car wash.

Meanwhile, Cumby's is out of "Royal Pine" and I may have to switch to "Red Spice".

5: THE TAXI TRADE 🚕

The Kingdom of Rathe's

The first thing is, you have to say it right. After all, this is a town where the Riverside Avenue truck dealer is known as "Charley-Boys". It's spelled "Charlesbois", and I've got to assume the correct pronunciation is something like "Shall-bwa". So, this is how you say it: "Ratty's".

Shawn, my long-time mechanic, gave me the bad news that the problem facing my taxi was a "bad T.V. cable". Uh-huh, right. In that I possess a mechanical ability roughly on par with that of an English springer spaniel, I wanted to tell him that — forget about TV — this car doesn't even have a CD player. It's sad that after so many years in the transportation business, I have never picked up — if only by pure osmosis — a working knowledge of auto mechanics. I checked myself, and asked, slightly less moronically, "Whatsa T.V. cable?"

"I'm sorry, Jernigan," he said, graciously leaving unsaid, "Excuse me for forgetting the astonishing breadth of your cluelessness." "It's the throttle valve. That's the problem you're having with the choppy acceleration. We gotta replace the throttle valve cable."

"Ah-ha," I said. "Of course, the throttle valve." Shawn was smiling at me like I'm an utterly transparent sixth grader. Thank goodness this is a man of complete integrity, or after all these years, he would probably own my furniture. "Is it an expensive part?" I asked.

"Well, put it this way. I think it would be worth your while to try to locate a used one at one of the junkyards. If you're up for it, Jernigan, why don't you try Rathe's?"

"Sure Shawn. I'll try Rathe's. That's that junkyard up to Colchester, towards Sunny Hollow, is that right?"

"Yeah, you got it," Shawn said. He gave me that whimsical smile again, and added, "Good luck."

Having lived up here for a score of years, and being a cabbie — and a nosy schmoozer of a cabbie, at that — I've garnered tons of stories on the greater Burlington area and its history. Granted, much of the received information is what you might call "dubious", still I assume most of what I hear to be at least in the vicinity of the truth, if not next-door neighbor to it. With this caveat, I recall a vague conversation about the Rathe property, something about it's early years as a hog farm, and some distant family patriarch being a local politico of no small weight. In any event, I've heard the junkyard sits on a huge parcel of prime Chittenden County land; it's said if the family ever decided to sell out to developers, they could expect a small fortune.

Up Route 7 I drove, past the second Winooski Interstate exit, past the Shaw's supermarket and all the other new development, until I took a left at a small green street sign reading, "Rathe Road". A little ways up was a red sign which said "Junkyard 1/2 mile ahead", under which was a thin white-painted arrow pointing down a road off to the right. At the beginning of this road was a sliding metal gate, quite formidable, almost Checkpoint Charley-ish. I half expected to see a few border soldiers in dull gray uniforms with sub-machine guns strapped to their backs. The gate was open and I continued on.

In the promised half-mile, I came upon a few small structures perched on a slight bluff. To the right was a nondescript tan building of boxy dimensions in front of which were stacked piles of used tires. Immediately ahead of me was a 35-foot, olive drab trailer with three white doors. A couple of cars were parked perpendicular to the trailer, so I pulled in and joined them.

The building was festooned with a number of signs, one of which listed the "rules" of the establishment. Of these rules, I recall only #4: "No alcohol or drug use in the junkyard." I contemplated Rule #4 for a few moments and thought, if not a junkyard, name me a more appropriate venue for alcohol and drug use?

I entered the trailer and took in the interior space. The bric-a-brac and assorted paraphernalia and wall hangings were instantly familiar: it was the old-fashioned look of a classic auto-related shop, be it repair, parts or collision. One fading calendar on the far wall had a photo of a woman with a blonde, Farah Fawcett hair-do, wearing hot pants and a halter posed in front of a classic Corvette Stingray. Something about that image made me long for a medium-rare porterhouse steak — don't ask me why.

At the other end of the room were three men, all smoking cigarettes. Country music played softly from an unseen radio. One barrel-chested older man sat behind a huge, oak desk, while two younger guys stood to the side. The seated man gave off the aura of Buddha-in-repose, and it was clear without asking that he was the Kahuna of this operation.

I slowly approached the desk, feeling not unlike Dorothy on her first encounter with the Wizard of Oz. I stopped maybe three feet before him and nodded. He nodded back. The setting was such that I expected him to then say, in a deep resonant tone, "Speak, my son." But he said nothing. I said, "Well, I need a T.V. cable," and went on to describe the year, make and model of my vehicle. I then added weakly, "Do you got one of those on hand?"

Silence. He was starting to freak me out. The large, watery eyes which had appeared so Buddha-like were now, on second thought, looking more like Jabba the Hutt's. He then rose from his ancient rolling office chair, and extended his right arm towards a rear door, and nodded once.

Great, I thought. In this rear addition to the trailer is where I'll find the parts counter, and the friendly and helpful parts-man, who will click my specs into his pastel-colored iMac computer, and then smiling, walk back into a warehouse, emerging moments later with my T.V. cable.

Not quite. Instead I walked through that rear door, and this is what I saw. I was back in the great outdoors from whence I came. Before me was a sprawling, endless field. As far as the eye could see were rows upon rows of junked cars, all in various stages of evisceration. I was stunned: this was the largest junkyard I had ever seen, the largest I could imagine.

I strode forth into this sea of metal, this flotilla of Volvos, Dodges and Hondas. The placement of the vehicles seemed entirely random: Saabs nestled Escorts; Pacers rubbed elbows with Mercedes. I wandered about for a little while searching for a match to my humble Plymouth. Then it occurred to me: if, by some miracle, I located a likely suspect, I would have no idea where to find the T.V. cable; if somehow I got past that hurdle, I would have no way of removing the T.V. cable.

I slunk back to my taxi — discretely circumnavigating the trailer on the way out — and drove back to my mechanic.

"Shawn," I said, walking onto his garage, "it was a good idea, but unfortunately Rathe's didn't have the part."

5: THE TAXI TRADE

Christopher Snow

While awaiting the evening Amtrak out in Essex Junction, I've taken to playing ball against the side of the station building. Recently, a company in Taiwan has begun producing "Spaldings", the pink rubber ball of my youth. What cost a quarter in the early '60's, is now sold to nostalgic baby boomers at Mills & Greer for $3.99. So I practice my curve ball, my slider, and spend the next day trying to ignore my aching shoulder and back. Such is middle-age.

At the bus stop next to the station one night in early July, I noticed a boy astride a BMX bicycle watching me intently. He rode over closer to me, and got off his bike.

"Hey Mister, do you know when the next bus is?" he asked, as I tossed another one against the wall. I snared the rebound and turned to face him directly.

"Yeah, I do," I said. "There's a bus at a quarter to nine. That's about 15 minutes from now."

"Thanks, Mister," he said, and stood there leaning against his bike.

He looked about nine or 10, with brown hair and thick bangs that fell just above round, dark eyes. His frame was lanky, and the size of his sneakers suggested he was due for a big growth spurt over the next year. There was a relaxed, open feeling in the way he held his body — no sign of the hardness or assumed swagger you see when the boys hit adolescence.

I recommended throwing the ball against the wall, as the kid, still watching, stood 10 feet to my left. Then I tossed it at an angle, so it caromed towards my new acquaintance. He caught it cleanly, threw it back at the wall, and I caught the rebound on a bounce. The two of us played this way for a few minutes, silent and grinning, the way guys do it.

"Hey, what's your name?" I asked, as I threw a hard one high up on the wall.

He back-pedaled a step and made a nice overhead catch of the big bounce. "Christopher Snow," he said. "You know, I rode here from Winooski."

"You don't say?" I replied. "That's a long ride. What street in Winooski d'ya live on?"

"I don't live in Winooski. I live in Missouri. I've been staying with my Mom and little brother in a hotel this summer. We came here to visit my Mom's boyfriend. She met him on the Internet."

"What about your Dad? Is he back in Missouri?"

"No, my Dad's dead. He died when I was little."

"That's too bad, Christopher." I held the ball in my hands for a moment before resuming the game. "What about your Mom's boyfriend? Is he an okay guy? D'ya like him?"

Christopher scrunched up his face, and now it was his turn to cup the ball and pause. It looked like he was seriously contemplating the question.

"Yeah, he's all right," he said. "He's real nice to my Mom. He bought me a *real* basketball. It has Kevin Garnet's name on it. You know, like he signed it!"

"That's great," I said. "There's nothing like a Kevin Garnet signature B-ball. He's a great player."

Christopher began our ball game again. Then he said, "You didn't ask me what I did today."

"I didn't? Jeez, I'm sorry. What did ya do today?"

"I played basketball with my friend, Nate, and then started ridin' our bikes. We rode all over the place. Nate's, like, hyper, so we just kept ridin' and ended up out here. Nate rode back to Winooski, but I got kinda tired. Some of the bus drivers know me and let me ride for free."

As if on cue, the Essex bus appeared at the end of the street. I took out my wallet.

"Christopher, here's a buck. You know, just in case this bus driver doesn't know you."

Christopher took the dollar and slid it into his trouser pocket. His pants hung low and baggy, the way the boys like them these days.

"Thanks, Mister," he said, and shot me a warm, crooked smile. I had a keen urge to pick him up and give him a long hug.

This kid is ready for life, I thought. Whether he ends up here, or back in Missouri, I had the strongest sense that he's going to do just fine. Still, I hoped — with a fierce intensity that surprised me — that the Internet guy had a heart big enough to see it through with Christopher and his family. It will be the lucky man, I thought, who gets to be Dad to this boy.

Christopher got back on his bike. I walked over to him and extended my hand. I said, "Good luck, Christopher. I'll see ya around."

He shook my hand shyly — gazing down a bit, then looking up sideways — but his grasp was firm for a small guy. God, it occurred to me, this kid must have one great Mom.

"Yeah, I'll see you, Mister," he said, and sped off to catch the bus.

6

The Very Cool

If you're a cabbie, a lifer like me, eventually you pick up some very cool people. Like, for instance, one night I drove Chubby Checker. (That's a story reserved for the second collection: Hackie 2: Jernigan's Revenge.) It's one of the few perks of the job — that and getting to park at all those taxi stands.

Living La Dolce Vita

There's nothing quite like the bustle of Perkin's Pier on a mid-August Saturday afternoon. The dock gently sways, seemingly breathing with the undulating movement of the lake water. The air is like nowhere else in the city: lightly scented with the pungent undertones of lake life. The ropes slap and clang against sailboat masts; various seabirds squawk, quack and coo; children laugh and run about the parked cars lined up for the next ferry.

What is it about water's edge that releases the insouciant spirit? I sure don't know, but I find myself coming down to work the ferry even though the pickings are usually slim. This summer scene is all too short-lived, and I just plain enjoy hanging out here.

"Are you free? Can you take us to the Sheraton?"

My reverie was broken by a woman standing by the window of my taxi. She was attractive, perhaps mid-thirties, and spoke with a heavy European accent.

"Sure," I replied. "That's pretty much what I do for a living."

"*Perfetto!*" she said. "Let me bring my three friends. I'll be right back."

I fired up the ignition, and watched her walk over to the slip occupied by a luxurious sailing vessel. If not quite the largest boat on the dock that day, it hovered on the water with a sleek and uncompromising magnificence, a step above all comers. She called, and two men and another woman disembarked to join her.

The men looked similar: both in their retirement years, with gracefully brushed-back silver hair. I was struck by their dress, which exuded a European elegance — all linen and relaxation. I was yet more struck by the other woman. Watching her slowly advance towards me, I caught myself blinking a few times. This was an exquisitely beautiful woman. She wore an off-white silk pants suit and an endless chartreuse scarf. The sheer love-liness of her face made me break into a dopey grin.

Before the group reached my cab, my mind had crunched the avail-able info-bits and spit out this assessment: These people were not Americans. Judging from the boat, clothes, *savoir-faire* and, of course, the accent, they were clearly Italians — and rich ones at that. Given the age differential, the women could be the daughters or nieces of the men. Not. If the men were American, I'd say we're looking at second, or third wives. Because they were Italian, the better guess was mistresses.

One of the gentlemen took the front seat, while the others settled into the back. My seatmate smiled at me benevolently, and I saw a kindness and acuity in his pale blue eyes.

As we got underway, I pulled a *USA Today* entertainment section off the dashboard. The main article concerned Sophia Loren, and featured a large color photo of her. I should explain that I love everything Italian — particularly Italians — and here I found myself with four beautiful ones. I guess I was feeling expansive and jolly.

"Look at this picture of Sophia!" I announced to all concerned. "Isn't she still fantastic? And what an actress! She can play comedy or drama. My goodness, *Two Women* — what a movie!"

"So true," the man in the back jumped in. "Not only that, but she can sing and dance."

Ah, the ball is rolling, I thought. The subject matter was irrelevant; I was thrilled merely to be conversing with bona fide Italians. I turned to speak to the man sitting next to me.

"And that was so sad to lose Marcello Mastroianni. Another great Italian actor. Those movies he made with Sophia will never be matched."

"Yes, I could not agree more," the man replied. He sighed and added wistfully, "I miss him so much. He was a good friend of mine."

I was about to shift to Roberto Benigni when his comment reached and registered in the cognitive brain cells.

"Did you say Marcello was a friend of yours? In what capacity, if I may ask, did you meet and know him?"

"Oh," he said off-handedly. "I wrote some movies he was in." There was not an ounce of ego in his voice, not a shred.

"Wow," I said. "You're a screenwriter."

"*Si, Si.* I write the movies."

"Now, you've never worked with Fellini, have you?" I don't know who was driving the cab at this point. Me, I suppose.

"Sure, yes I have," he replied. "Very often."

"Any films I might have seen?"

"Well," he replied. "I worked on *La Dolce Vita.*"

Ronzoni Sono Buoni! This is it, I thought. I've hit the Italian mother lode.

"Now, I'm really amazed," I said. "That's got to be one of the greatest movies of all times. I *love* that movie. What was Fellini like? His films are filled with such wonder and awe."

"Just like that," he answered. "Federico was just like his movies. With the heart and eyes of a child. No, there will not be another like Federico."

Just then, I pulled the taxi up to the Sheraton entrance. My customers all stepped out, and the screenwriter removed a suede wallet from his jacket pocket. He leaned in through the front door to pay the fare. Suddenly, he gazed skyward with a far-away look.

"Federico's wife! *Stupenda*! What a magnificent cook. *Fantastica*! I can still smell her food, I can taste it!"

He then began to recount, in Italian, the favorite dishes of Mrs. Fellini — the actress Giulietta Masina. His arms and hands sculpted air with mesmerizing finesse, his fingers providing all the punctuation. I understood barely a word, yet I sat in rapt attention.

His eyes were twinkling as he got to one special dish — *scallopini* something — and my mouth began to water. Right then and there, in front of the Sheraton Burlington, I enjoyed my most delicious meal ever, courtesy of a great Italian screenwriter.

She's Got the Way to Move Me, Cherie

A Thursday evening finds me idling at the St. Paul and Main taxi stand. I sense an energy, some commotion over my left shoulder. Passing the Flynn Theater heading west is a small congregation of people. I observe they are all men, and grouped in a diamond-like formation, like the smallest unit of a Roman legion advancing into battle. The greatest number — perhaps five or six abreast — stride shoulder-to-shoulder in the center of this configuration; the rest taper off towards the front and rear.

This is one animated group, I think, as I watch them gesturing, laughing, almost dancing down Main Street. Then I notice a statuesque woman in the center of the swarm — the queen bee, as it were. She towers above her minions; how could I have initially missed her?

Holy smokes! — it hits me in a flash — it's Cherie Tartt!

Up until that moment, I'd only seen Cherie on that cable TV show she hosts with her cohort, Yolanda. Men who impersonate women have never intrigued me, yet I always quit surfing when Cherie and Yolanda pop up on the screen.

In these days of ubiquitous irony — it's practically the subtext of an entire generation — Cherie and Yolanda take it to a another, higher stratosphere. The two of them are so effortlessly sardonic, so gleefully wry, that the irony does a turnaround: Rather than coming across as cynical or mean-spirited, the two of them strike me as exuberantly cheerful. Plus, they are hilarious together, and the entire show, as far as I can tell, is totally improvised before the camera.

If you've ever watched the show, you know that, between the two stars, Cherie is the "demure" one, sweetly reining in the bursting-out-of-the-seams Yolanda. Her role is something of the straight man, though referring to Cherie as a "straight man" in any context seems singularly ludicrous. The shtick is a sight to behold — right up there with George &

Gracie, or Regis & Kathy Lee. But *sans* Yolanda, Cherie in the flesh — and, Gadzooks! here she is — extinguishes any notion of the shrinking violet.

Sashaying across Main Street before my eyes, Cherie appears about 6'3" if she's an inch; with the boost of her high heels, the overall effect is Junoesque. As she crosses directly in front of the cab, her ultra-bouffant hair-do appears beyond pink, like some celestial cotton candy. Her black dress is a sleeveless number with spaghetti straps, and I kid you not, her legs are not half-bad.

I would venture that even in New York City or Boston, where there are many such . . . how to put this . . . extravagantly expressed people, Cherie would stand out and cause a stir. But here in little old Burlington, our very own Queen City, she's a living landmark.

Within earshot of my cab, I hear a passerby loudly mutter, "Goddam faggots! What the hell is this town coming to?"

I can't tell if the Cherie pack heard this insult too, but if so, I can't imagine it's an unaccustomed event. Even in relatively open-minded Vermont, a man can't publicly dress like a woman without provoking a certain amount of flak.

What's the button being pushed, I wonder? It's got to be something visceral to incite such hate, even violence on occasion. Maybe gay bashers are expressing, in skewed fashion, a hatred of women. Within their sulphurous view of the world, do they see gays, and in particular, female impersonators, as traitors to their gender? As if a man, by virtue of simply donning a dress, has "gone over to the other side" in some perceived gender war?

An analogy is racists who reserve their greatest ire for white people who have in some way become close to the black community.

An audible sigh escapes from deep within my chest. Theorize, analyze, speculate; no matter how you cut it, it's depressing to ponder hate.

Entering City Hall Park, the entourage is in high gear, fluttering about their leading lady like honeybees around a rose bush. Cherie is calm and self-possessed as she whispers to one or another of the lucky ones, giggles, and then throws her head back in delighted laughter. All of this, as I said, I'm taking in from my taxicab box seat while parked on the corner.

Suddenly, the grande dame turns her face ever so slightly to the right, and I swear she's looking right at me! Her wafer lips, magenta red, register the faintest indication of pleasure. Her almond eyes, dark and watery like Burlington bay on a moonlit night, gaze out at me with a sublime mischievousness. She blinks once, and her luxuriant eyelashes shimmer with what looks like sugar frosting. For one evanescent moment, I feel as if in communion with the Mona Lisa's flamboyant sister.

The moment passes — could it have been my fertile imagination? my wishful thinking? — and she's off gliding towards Church Street, a one-woman, traveling show.

Till next time, my Cherie. Thanks for being out there, and thanks for lighting up this town.

The New Age Nurses
Give Me the Treatment

Some colleges develop an extensive summer program. For instance, Middlebury College's summer language and writing programs are nationally acclaimed and well-attended. The University of Vermont has not gone this route. Instead, in an effort to generate at least some revenue from the "physical plant" while the students are away, the UVM campus is the host site for a steady stream of summer conferences, symposiums and sundry gatherings. From Guitar Making to Recent Developments in Microbiology, various groups find a hospitable and practical setting at UVM.

The five women I picked up at the Sweetwater's corner were in town for a week-long seminar titled, "Bringing Holistic Methods to the Nursing Profession". The sixtyish gray-haired woman who sat up front with me appeared to be their informal leader. She wore a plain white shift dress, simple sandals, and her hair was up in a makeshift bun with tendrils falling off to each side of her temples. It was quite a becoming look.

She introduced herself as June, and told me a little about the seminar that had brought her and her colleagues to Burlington. Apparently, research is increasingly demonstrating the effectiveness of various methods of non-conventional healing methods such as prayer, guided meditation, herbalogy, and the like. Many nurses are interested in learning about these techniques and introducing them to the medical settings in which they work. Hence, this seminar.

The energy level among these five women was unique in my experience. Their talking, giggling and sharing was enlivening. I felt a palpable rise in my spirits during just the 10-minute ride to campus. June told me the conference was drawing to a close, but they planned on going out one more time tomorrow night. I gave her my card and she said they would be sure to call.

The following day, I was in a terrible mindset. I was disheartened, disconsolate and slightly headachy to boot. The world was clearly getting the best of me. When June called for a ride back to campus that night (they must have walked downtown earlier), I was in no mood for human contact. My attitude was: Just let me stew.

Against all probability, the five nurses were glowing with even more intensity than the previous night.

"The final workshop had been on 'Cleansing the Human Aura'," June explained in a musical voice. "The aura, you see, is the subtle energy field which surrounds every person. When people speak of halos, this may be what's being perceived. Like a white t-shirt, the aura can become soiled or stained, and in the workshop we learned a technique — like Tide and a Maytag — to clean the aura right up!"

"Okay. That's great, June. Now leave me alone."

I didn't actually say this, but no doubt, I viscerally projected such bad vibes. June immediately picked up on my state of mind. In a quiet, non-pushy tone, she said, "You look like you're having a rough day. How about when we get back to the dorms, we do an aura cleansing on you? What do you say, girls?" The four nurses squeezed in the back heartily agreed.

"Bah, humbug," my mind grumbled. "I don't need no stinkin' treatment." I heard my voice say, "Sure, I'd love it."

Back at the Harris-Millis dorms, I parked the taxi and got out. One nurse located a plastic folding chair and set it up in a small grassy area. June instructed me to sit in the chair, and "just relax". I could keep my eyes open or closed, "whatever's more comfortable". Under normal circumstances I would have approached this endeavor with not just a little trepidation. But these bright-eyed women exuded so much — well, love — that I felt totally safe in whatever was about to transpire.

With half-closed eyes, I watched the nurses form into a circle surrounding me. With open palms turned toward me, they began to move their hands in a rubbing motion about one or two feet from my body. If my skin extended out a foot and a half in every direction, they would have been gently caressing me. I then closed my eyes entirely, and it felt somehow like I was actually being caressed. The sensation was warm and cool simultaneously. I was overwhelmed by the deep expression of caring being shown by these strangers. As the treatment progressed, I felt lighter, less troubled.

The whole process took less than five minutes. When I opened my eyes, they were all looking at me, beaming like light bulbs. I got up and they each gave me a hug. I felt like Dorothy at the end of *The Wizard of Oz* when she bids farewell to the Lion, Tinman and Scarecrow. It was like, "June, I'm going to miss you most of all." It was that sappy and touching.

Reflecting on this extraordinary experience, the words of J.D. Salinger come to mind. One of his characters called himself a "reverse paranoiac". And this is also how it seems to me: The world is continually conspiring to make me happy.

The Odd Couple

I stood in the baggage arrival area with two customers, Joseph Fuentes and Arthur Gravelin, both men in their sixties and bound for the same board meeting at the Sugarbush Inn. Beyond that, they couldn't have been more different.

One gentleman, Mr. Gravelin, was visibly perspiring in a dark blue, three-piece suit, his bifocals perched on the tip of his nose. Periodically, he pulled back on a head of oily black hair with a cupped hand. It seemed like he was checking his watch every 30 seconds. I don't know if the waiting time is atypical for larger, metropolitan airports, but at Burlington Airport, you can cool your heels for up to a half-hour between disembarkment and luggage arrival.

His associate, Mr. Fuentes, was dressed in airy cotton, or perhaps linen pants of a neutral gray-brown hue, with a similar shirt and open vest. He was bald in the front, with fine silver hair brushed back and slightly curling at the collar. His eyes were round, clear, sky-blue, and, as I glanced at him, strikingly tranquil. Although not obviously muscular, he seemed to move from the center of his abdomen, with a strength and power unusual for a man his age. His body emanated, if that's the word, a peaceful, soothing vibration. I found myself wanting to stare at him, such was his low-key charisma.

The red warning light went on, and the luggage handlers behind the back wall sounded the buzzer three times, signaling the start of the conveyor belt. Even taking into account the high density of ambient noise in the terminal building, the signal volume was clearly overkill; the ear-piercing razz would be more appropriate to incoming nuclear attack, not the imminent arrival of encased clothing and toiletries. I mean, no need to wake the dead; they already have their luggage.

The children in the room, already amply jazzed from either the thrill of flying or meeting a plane, burst with new excitement as the luggage began to circle.

My customers and I stood around watching the belt, waiting for the men's pieces. It felt like the right time for some temperate repartee, perhaps, "Where did you fly from?" or "Is this your first visit to Vermont?" Forgoing the formality, I cut to the chase.

I turned towards Mr. Fuentes. "Are you an athlete of some kind?" I asked. This was a lame version of what I really wanted to ask, namely, "Who *are* you? A Jedi Knight?"

He chuckled, and replied, " No, I'm no longer a competitive athlete, if that's what you're asking. I did compete in the Olympics in judo, during the last cycle before it became an official Olympic sport. I still teach judo out of my home in Monterey."

"I thought so," I said. "There was something about the way you move."

I was unnerving myself with this degree of forwardness. I'm decidedly an extrovert, but I generally manage to maintain a touch more decorum with people I've just met. Mr. Fuentes's smiling acknowledgement, however, assured me he was unfazed by my comments.

The bags came around, and we snaked out of the terminal, loaded up the taxi and headed out, destination Warren. The men sat together in the back. It was evident that they knew each another well enough to talk personally. Despite personas as disparate as Oscar and Felix, there was a warmth to their conversation.

"So, Joe, tell me — how's life in Monterey? How do you spend your days since you retired?"

"Well, the mornings are devoted to my judo practice and meditation. I've told you about the property, haven't I? I've built a new wing off the main house where I teach my classes in the early afternoon. Late afternoon, I work at the poetry. My publisher expects the new collection by summer's end."

"What kind of poetry do you write?" I shamelessly butted in from the front.

"It's free-form, in the tradition of William Blake and the Indian poets. Sometimes it's referred to as 'ecstatic poetry'."

"My God, Joe," Mr. Gravelin piped in. "What a schedule! You are the most disciplined son-of-a-gun I've ever known. I don't know how you do it — I really don't."

"All of it just keeps me out of trouble, Artie. If I really had any guts, I'd do what you do. You're still at it, aren't you?"

"Wouldn't stop for the world," Mr. Gravelin replied, and for the first time, I saw his eyes light up in whimsy.

Now I was really curious. From the moment I laid eyes on him, I had Mr. Gravelin pegged as squarely stick-in-the-mud. And here was the other guy — a world-class judo master, living in luxury in Monterey, California, composing "ecstatic" poetry (which gets published — a miracle for any poet) — expressing envy towards this apparent schlemiel. Even saying he's being generous to a friend, what could Mr. Gravelin be up to that evokes such admiration?

In the rear-view mirror, I saw Mr. Fuentes give his seatmate a gentle poke in the arm. "C'mon, Artie — why don't you tell our cabdriver what you've taken up in retirement?"

Mr. Gravelin straightened a bit in his seat, and said, "I'm a clown."

"Did you say, 'clown'?" I asked incredulously.

"I did. I'm a clown in the Big Apple Circus. In fact, up until this year, we've performed at your Shelburne Museum every summer."

"Well, knock me over with a feather," I replied. "That's, well . . . *amazing* is what it is."

My mind works like a high school test essay — compare, contrast and draw a conclusion. Here was the juicy question that occupied my thoughts for the rest of the trip: *Who had the more meaningful vocation — the crouching tiger, or the hidden jester?*

Wild Colonials
at the Colonial!

These early October weeks are among the busiest of the entire year. Between foliage tourists, student revelers, business conferences, and parents' weekends at the colleges — we cabbies are running on fumes. There's money on the streets, but it's hard-earned.

On a recent Saturday night, amidst the autumn hubbub, I was hailed by a tall blonde-haired man. In a town with its share of colorful characters, this guy was making his own striking statement.

Like a hip-hop producer who borrows styles and snippets from older songs creating something new, this man appeared to have sampled fashion themes from years gone by. But rather than coming off as old-fashioned or retro, he looked entirely original — fresh and unpretentious. The two parts of his ensemble that immediately drew my gaze were the plaid pants and Russian fur hat. The hat recalled the headdress of Graham Nash in the early days of his association with Crosby and Stills.

I pulled the cab to a stop; he approached my window.

"I need to pick up my friend at Nectar's," he said. "Will that be all right?"

He got in the back, and we turned into a spot in front of the night club. Waiting there was a woman with the darkest black hair, which extended out from a blue woolen cap, spilling down the sides of her face in comely tight ringlets. Like her friend, her attire was splendid and unusual. Next to her, tucked back against the building wall, sat a violin case, a small amp and some other electronic-looking gear.

"Angela," the man called out from his cracked window, "get in the taxi. I'll get the equipment."

Angela climbed into the front seat, as the man was getting out. I popped the trunk.

"D'ya want some help now, Paul," Angela asked. Her Scottish brogue was musical and lilting, like an old folk song.

"No, my dear, it's not much," Paul replied. "I can handle it."

Angela then turned to me and smiled a bright, friendly smile.

Of course, it hit me: these people are performers. No, this was not more of that "psychic cabbie" business, just simple deduction from the obvious evidence.

"Did you guys play here tonight?" I asked.

"Yes, we sure did," Angela replied.

"What name do you perform under? I mean, are you a band?"

Paul was just getting into the rear seat, and heard the question. "We're the Wild Colonials," he said.

"Yowzah!" I said. "I've heard of you guys. They've been playing your music a lot on the radio up here. Where can I take you? Where are you staying?"

Angela turned to look at Paul, and let out a guffaw. "Believe it or not," she said, "we're staying at the Colonial."

I laughed out loud, also a guffaw. "That *is* hilarious," I said, as I backed out and headed the vehicle south.

"So how's the band doing?" I asked. "Have you opened for any big acts?" My nosiness knows no bounds. Actually, I've been working overtime to rein it in, but given this circumstance, I wrote myself a pass. I love bands and I love musicians.

Paul said, "You bet we have," and proceeded, with Angela's help, to rattle off a half-dozen of the biggest groups of the moment. Angela then added, "And we've been recording with Cyndi Lauper."

"All right!" I said, surrendering the last shred of pretense of being cool and unimpressed. "I love Cyndi's music. Those tunes from the eighties — I mean, 'Time After Time', I still tear up when I hear that."

Angela smiled warmly, nodding her head in agreement with the sentiment.

"You know," I continued, "Cyndi attended college here in Vermont, at Johnson State, if I got it straight."

"No kidding," Angela said. "She never told me that one." She paused for a moment, and then appeared to make up her mind about something. She then pivoted in her seat to face her band mate. "Paul, give me the tape," she said.

Paul said, "Are you sure, Angela?"

"You bet; it feels right," she said, and then turned to me.

"You got a working tape player there, man?" she asked. "Play this tape. It's a song Cyndi and I wrote together. This is the demo we recorded a few nights ago. You're going to be the first person to hear it."

I took the tape from her hand, and slid it into the deck. Just then we came to the Colonial Motor Inn, and I took the left into the parking lot.

"D'ya have time to just stop and listen?" I asked.

"Sure, man," Angela replied. "If you do, we do. Let's listen."

The ringing strum of a twelve-string guitar began the song. It was a slow, folksy ballad. Cyndi Lauper came in on the first verse. Her tremulous, heart-achy voice is like no other, and she sounded beautiful and true.

On the chorus, Angela joined in, and it was startling. She could have been Cyndi's twin sister: the two voices were that harmonious and identical in tone. The song went on, telling us a story of longing and loss. The two women traded verses and harmonies. It was a gorgeous tune, and I was literally shivering at my chance fortune in getting to hear it.

When the final echo of the lone guitar receded, I popped out the tape and handed it back to Angela.

"That was really, really beautiful," I said. As usual, any dose of eloquence had deserted me when I truly needed it. "Thank you so much for playing it for me."

Angela's Scottish eyes were sparkling. "The tune is called, 'Behind the Sun', she said, "and it's going to be the title track of a movie by the same name. Don't be askin' me when it's being released, but glory be, we got the title song!"

This is why I stick to hacking: every fare is an adventure. In the greater scheme of things, I suppose the Queen City is a cultural backwater, but it attracts some cool and remarkable people. And when I'm lucky, they need a cab.

Hey, Toots!

"Hey, man, couldja wait a minute? I got someone comin' out for ya — he needs to get to the Clarion."

The bouncer — all six-and-a-half feet of him — had hailed me over to the entrance of a downtown club. It was early evening, and kind of early for them to be open, I thought to myself.

A few minutes later, a striking black woman with gorgeous, intricately-beaded braids exited the club, followed by a middle-aged man wearing a colorful dashiki-like shirt. I immediately figured them for musicians. Casually — with show biz types you want to be cool — I asked them if they were in town for a concert.

"Not me, mon" the woman answered. "But dis 'ere is Toots. De Maytals be playin' in town tonight and tomorrow."

Toots, of Toots and the Maytals! My heart stepped up a beat. As a young teenager, I recall listening to the landmark reggae album, the soundtrack to *The Harder They Come*, which featured a number of pioneer reggae performers. My favorite tune on that record was the bouncy, hypnotic "Pressure Drop" by the Maytals.

It's an odd sensation, meeting in the flesh a person whose creative works are part of your consciousness, a fixture in your inner dream world. Hacking has afforded me the opportunity to meet a number of recording artists while they were gigging in Burlington, including Dave Brubeck, Chubby Checker, Jerry Lee Lewis and Keith Jarrett, to name but a few. All of those brushes with celebrity came in handy with Toots, because I managed to speak to him with a minimum of blubbering, non-sequiturs.

"Toots," I said, "I'm thrilled to meet you. Your music has meant a great deal to me."

'Mon, dat's just great," he replied. "It's good to be wit you. You 'ahv tickets to de show, mon? Darlene, baby, let's comp dis cabbie-mon."

His warmth felt like the sun. Here's a guy in the public eye for at least 40 years. After that long, you would forgive him a blasé reaction to praise from a fan. His response, amazingly, was the opposite of jaded — his sincerity was palpable. I felt as if my appreciative words genuinely touched him. It was like he had sent you some love via his music, and receiving it back was, to him, a meaningful part of the creative process. I gratefully accepted a couple of passes for the next night's show, and Toots arranged for a noon pick up the next day. "Me 'ahv some tings to get done, mon," he told me.

First stop the following day was Greer's Cleaners, all part of life on the road for a working musician. The three of us entered the store and Toots plopped a small bundle of clothing on the counter. Darlene did the talking. It seemed as if she functioned as combination girlfriend, personal assistant and spiritual advisor.

"We 'ahv a show tonight, missus," she explained to the woman behind the counter. Her voice was soft and respectful. "Do you tink you folks can 'ahv it ready by six o'clock?"

The counter lady was a typical stoic Vermonter, yet her eyes emitted a noticeable sparkle. How often does she wait on a black couple with the bearing and attire of Caribbean royalty?

"Yup," she replied. "We can do that. You want the shirts boxed or on a hanger?"

Next it was on to the health food store to pick up some herbs and teas. Apparently, Toots was recovering from recent appendicitis surgery and Darlene was keeping him on a restorative diet. His doctors had strongly advised against touring for at least four months, a prescription it seemed Toots never seriously considered.

"De music is what heals me, mon," Toots told me as we pulled into the parking lot. "Wit'out singin' me songs, I will never get strong again."

As we walked toward the door, a young couple dressed in similar, patch-work flannel, with blond dreadlocks tumbling over their shoulders, recognized Toots. This was not surprising. Charisma is too weak a word to describe the man's presence. It's as if he had absorbed the Jamaican sun into his very core, and it now surrounded his body as a pale yellow glow. It didn't appear to be anything he consciously evoked or projected; it was simply his being's essence.

"Wow, we saw you last night, Toots," the young man excitedly poured out. "You were the bomb, man. We love you."

As he had reacted with me the previous day, Toots smiled broadly at his two young fans.

"Keep do love strong, me friends," he said. "Dis is what de reggae music is all 'bout." In his two hands he clasped first the guy's and then the girl's hands, and we continued into the store.

While shopping, Darlene mentioned they were getting hungry, and I suggested the Caribbean restaurant off Pearl Street. I'm acquainted with the owner, and I knew bringing Toots over to his place would make his week, if not his life. Unfortunately, it was closed when we arrived, so went to the Indian place next door. Toots insisted that I join them. Frankly, it didn't take much arm-twisting — Indian is my favorite cuisine, and I was thoroughly enjoying the company.

Once seated, Toots asked me what was good, and proceeded to order everything I mentioned, and a few things more. The table filled up with curries, tandoori breads, and sweet and spicy condiments. I got the impression that he basically ate one meal a day, so it was a doozy.

Over lunch I asked Toots about his life in music. He spoke with love, yet as he recounted the early years, there was the unmistakable flavor of bittersweet, if not plain bitter.

"It was me and Bob, mon," he said between bites. "We invented dis music. It was me who named it 'reggae'. But de record company give me no support, mon. None. It was all Bob Marley. Him dey push and push."

This is an interesting point, I thought. As a peer of the late Bob Marley, Toots faced the dilemma of comparison with one of the greatest songwriters of the 20th Century — an inspirational cultural icon on par with John Lennon and Bob Dylan. Toots made, and continues to make, a happy, soulful sound. But Bob Marley's music and message invoked a higher realm — moving listeners' hearts and minds, changing lives. For contemporary Jamaican artists like Toots, I could see how difficult it would be to resist the green genie.

The food kept coming. Occasionally Darlene would admonish Toots to avoid a particular dish, to which he would tease her, grumble and ultimate accede to her wishes. As the desserts were brought out — and there was no skimping here either — Toots decided to order an additional throng of dishes to go, "For after de show". Darlene carried the money, so she paid the check.

We returned to the hotel, and Toots asked me if I was going to the show tonight.

"Wouldn't miss it for the world," I replied. "Look for me in the audience."

That night the joint was humming when the Maytals, *sans* Toots, broke into their opening number, "Pressure Drop". I've heard many bands play the unique reggae beat; indeed, it's been absorbed into the pastiche of sounds and styles that define rock and roll. But the quality of the Maytals' reggae was like hearing it for the first time. it was so pure, so thick and expressive that you could walk on it.

Everyone in the crowd was bouncing and cheering when Toots took the stage, resplendent in multi-colored matching dashiki and pants. He began to jump up and down in time to the rhythm, and you could feel the energy level in the room double. After a few minutes of this, a calm frenzy settled over the crowd, and only then did Toots lift the mike to his mouth and roar out the opening lyric: "It is you — oh yeah, yeah, yeah."

Maybe Toots' music will never spark social revolution, but making people feel this good — there's something powerful and sacred to that as well. Bob Marley I have no doubt, is up there serenading the angels, and for all I know, is sitting right at the side of Haile Selassie, the Rastafarian patriarch. But that night, I bet Bob was smiling down at his old friend, Toots.

Bizarrerie

At least monthly, a customer asks, "Hey, cabbie. What's the craziest fare you ever had?" It's always hard for me to pick one, but fun to review the prime candidates.

Ten Easy Pizzas

It was the tail end of a long Friday night. The take had been good and I had earned it; week in and week out Friday nights are the busiest and craziest. Now it was 3:40 A.M. and I swung one last time through the bar district, trolling for a late straggler. Only then would I call it a night.

Out of Manhattan Pizza emerged two older, rumpled gentlemen. One of them wore a crumpled Rex Harrison hat, and the other, despite the summer weather, sported a blue blazer with some manner of British crest-of-arms on the breast pocket. They might just as well have worn embroidered signs on their backs saying "Fuddy-Duddies, Inc." They appeared pretty well lit up and were moving gingerly, with that exaggerated step of the intoxicated. Each one carried, platter-style in his arms, a stack of five cardboard pizza boxes.

This sighting was unusual on two fronts. First, by this time of night, all but the twenty-somethings have long since packed it in, to say nothing of the sixty-somethings. Second, what's up with the ten pizzas? And then — my goodness — they hailed me.

"To the Radisson, my good man," spake the blue blazer man as I pulled to the curb.

How does a porcupine make love? Carefully, which is exactly the manner in which two besotted, ten-pie transporting seniors enter a taxi. After a slow, deliberate ingress, landing and settling in, Rex Harrison was planted to my right, and blue blazer in the rear.

"The girls are going to love this, don't you think Alfred?" my seat mate said to his associate in the back.

"Without a question," replied Alfred. "A hot pizza surprise is just the thing, Spike, just the thing." (*Spike?!*)

What was intriguing to begin with had become genuinely piquant. Now, I thought, if only I can figure this out in the quarter-mile hop to the

Radisson. In order to gain a few extra observational minutes, I decided to proceed serpentine-style *en route*.

"These pies smell lovely, do they not, young man?" Spike was speaking to me — me being the only human in the vehicle vaguely qualifying as a "young man". The steam coming off the sauce and cheese had permeated the taxi, and was indeed mouth-watering, particularly since I hadn't a bite to eat going back to a late lunch.

"Sir, with all due respect, I fear 'lovely' is woefully insufficient." (Why was I suddenly speaking as if I was in an English drawing room comedy?) "The smell, if I might, is positively *luscious*."

"Well, Spike, that settles it," Alfred said, "I think we ought to give him a pie."

"Precisely my thought," replied Spike as he passed me the top pie from his stack.

Last year, a guy gave me a fifty-keep-the-change on a $12 fare to Williston. That was sweet, but for sheer tastiness, this was the best tip I'd ever received from a customer.

As I pulled into the Radisson entrance, five or six beautiful young women in slinky, slit skirts and tank tops rushed to the taxi.

"Oh Spike, you think of everything" and "Alfred, you are simply the best" — and other such sentiments filled the air. Apparently the early-morning pizza party concept had hit all the right chords. Into the hotel sauntered our dashing duo, a woman on each arm, with one to spare.

Your guess is as good as mine. To this day, I've never figured this one out, though don't think my imagination has not performed triple axels in the attempt.

Meanwhile the 4:00 A.M. church bells began their toll, and I was in possession of a large, mushroom pizza, which might very well be extra-cheese. Lifting the cover, I hoisted a slice, folded it and downed it in four massive bites. Chewing — the civilizing process of mastication which distinguishes us from our Neanderthal forbearers — was not part of the equation. Another piece shortly met the same fate. Partially sated, I gazed down at the remaining six — a pie-chart illustrating the notion of three-quarters — and upon me came the altruistic urge to share the bounty.

At the corner of Main and Church, a gaggle of police officers congregated under the preternatural glow of a sodium streetlight. They seemed in good spirits, and I pulled over and leaned towards the passenger window.

"Any of you officers in the mood for some pizza? A customer just tipped me a whole pie."

The tallest of the blue-folk walked over to the cab. His moustache defined "handlebar".

"Thank you very much for the offer, but we can't take food from civilians," he said, not stiffly though not exactly warmly.

I've never in my life uttered the phrase, "Suit yourself", but it almost slipped out in that moment. What overkill, I thought. How much police favoritism do they think you can you buy for a slice of pizza?

Glancing down the street, I noticed a couple of guys going through the trash can in front of the Rusty Scuffer. They were deposit-bottle hunters and doing quite well from the looks of their nearly-filled supermarket cart. I pulled onto Church and called to them: "You guys want some pizza?"

"Right on, brother!" came the instantaneous reply from the one of the pickers, who was wearing sky-blue overalls. The bottle-hunter's union apparently contains no protocol against pizza gifts from civilians. "What kind do you got there?"

"I got mushroom, and it may or may not be extra-cheese."

"Let's do it up then!" the second picker bellowed.

With that, the three of us took seats on the outdoor benches and finished off the six slices. They were appreciative of the largesse and I was appreciative of the company. I can't recall a better evening-topper than this one.

Fried Green Oldsmobiles

In our region, most taxi fares originate and terminate within the immediate Burlington area. When you take someone to an outlying town — Milton, Underhill, Monkton, et. al. — you fully expect to return empty. Bagging a return fare in these situations is gravy — pure, thick, savory Nectar's Diner gravy. But sometimes you ask the prettiest girl to the dance and she says, "Yes", and sometimes you get the gravy. It could happen.

I just dropped a fare at the cheese factory in Hinesburg, and returning north on 116, I spot a large green vehicle on the roadside, hood raised. An older man is hunched over the engine. As I draw close, he waves me down.

"I'm out of gas," he says. "Where's the nearest station?"

"This time of night that would be the Mobil up on Gracey's Corner," I reply.

"Let's do it, partner," he says.

All right! Gimme gravy with my mashed potatoes!

The man climbs in, and right away, I like him. You know how it is — sometimes you just like somebody. His hair is pure fifties, he looks to be in his sixties and his attire is vintage seventies. Remember Wayne Cochran and the C.C. Riders? This guy is channeling Wayne. High pompadour white as snow, and though it's still quite cold, he's wearing only a "leisure suit" (there's an oxymoronic phrase) over a ruffled white shirt, white as his hair. The "suit" color, God help me, is mauve. As the French — a wordy, articulate bunch if there ever was one — put it: *chacun à son goût* — everyone to his own taste. This guy isn't merely a piece of work, he's an entire work unto himself, and he hits the seat talking.

"Goddam Oldsmobiles! I thought those Japanese mothers forced GM to make cars that work! Can't even design a goddam gas gauge to work right."

Never mind that his car dates back to the Watergate hearings. I think he's lucky the pistons are still pumping.

"Where are you from, Buddy?" I ask. "Somewhere down south, I bet."

"You got that right, partner," he replies. "The name's Clyde by the way. I'm from Nashville. I'm up here visiting my sister's family in Starksboro. Boy, she wasn't kidding about the weather. It's colder'n hell up here."

I've been living in Vermont long enough now to have internalized the propensity to talk endlessly about the weather. And enjoy it, no less. Thusly, Clyde and I chat meteorologically, as well as about this, about that, and about the other thing. Never have I enjoyed a more amiable conversation traveling up Hinesburg Road.

Arriving at the all-night gas station, Clyde does the gas can deposit thing, and now we're heading back. Presumably in about 15 minutes we'll be back at his vehicle, he'll pay the fare (with hopefully a good tip), pour the gallon of gas into the empty gas tank, hit the ignition (vroom-vroom) and all is copasetic.

However, when we reach his car, Clyde doesn't pay me right away. Rather, he asks me to wait to make sure the engine will indeed start. He puts the gas in, cranks the ignition and it won't turn over. I watch him make a number of futile attempts at this until he gets out, opens the trunk and fishes out a blue plastic container. As he walks over to me, I see the container says, "Starter Fluid".

"Okay," Clyde says. "Here's the deal. I'll try to start her up again while you squirt this stuff on the carburetor."

I confess I'm not much of a car mechanic. Actually, that's giving me too much credit. I'm not a car mechanic, period. That said, I trust my intuition, and my gut says, "This is a bad thing."

This assessment is affirmed as I take the starter fluid from Clyde, and notice the prominent warning label: "For use on small engines such as snowmobiles, lawnmowers, etc. Not recommended for use on automobiles." I point this out to Clyde.

"Well," he says. "That just shows you can't believe everything you read, partner, I can't tell you how many times I've started a car with this stuff. Never once had a problem."

What the hell do I know? Clyde gets behind the wheel and gives me the thumbs-up sign, like John Glenn at lift-off. Clyde cranks. I squirt. He cranks. I squirt. Nothing.

He leans out the window, pompadour first. "C'mon, put some oomph into it. It ain't fine wine."

Got it. He again hits the ignition. I squeeze with both palms, shooting a thick stream directly onto the carb.

"Clyde, how's —" That's all I get out, because at that instant, the engine is engulfed in flame. Not a sputtering camp cookfire, but huge, four-foot, orange, yellow and red spikes higher than eye level.

I leap away from the car. There's nothing like fire to focus your attention. They should try it at Zen retreats, I think. I'm standing by the taxi which is parked on the opposite shoulder. Clyde, so help me, is still in the driver's seat trying to start the engine.

"Clyde!" I yelp. "Get the hell outta there!" Are you nuts!?"

"Shaddup!" comes back. This guy apparently is in Captain of the Titanic mode — he's going down with the ship.

Meanwhile, the flames have abated not one iota. This thing can blow at any moment. Survival takes over. The lizard brain, located, I'm told, somewhere behind and south of the navel screams, "We're outta here!" I jump into the taxi and gun it.

About a hundred yards up the road and still accelerating, I glance at my rear-view and get this last image of the scene: The green, monstrous boat of a car, engine ablaze. I'm not sure, but I swear I can spot the white pompadour bobbing up and down through the flames and the windshield.

So much for the gravy.

Nudie on Duty

There's that long stretch after the foliage has its final say. Winter is lurking behind every wind-swept downtown building, like a lumbering, white polar bear stretching its muscles, groaning and calling from the near distance.

Inevitably, winter closes in. The wardrobe simplifies. The Sorels and winter coat are the everyday choice; the only decision is which pair of gloves and how many sweaters?

Now it's early January, and the bear has arrived. I'm idling on a Thursday night at a downtown taxi stand. There's no shutting it down to save gas anymore; winter nights demand a non-stop purring heater.

For us cabbies, the cold weather is a mixed blessing. On the plus side, there are more fares. People don't want to walk even short distances in a deep freeze, nor do they relish awaiting the bus, or even driving their own cars — *if* they start — when it's snowy. On the minus side, we cabbies get worn down by the mental strain of hours sliding around treacherous roads. Of course, here in Vermont, brutal winter conditions are the third inevitability, right after death and taxes. Why complain about the ineluctable?

Gossamer flurries begin swirling in wavy circles over the black asphalt. I find myself drifting back to a favorite warm-weather memory. Firmly placed in my top five taxi moments of the new century is the Night of the Nudie Cyclists . . .

. . . It was the last week of classes and the graduating seniors were feeling frisky. Some brilliant *summa cum laude* must have come up with the idea — the sort of plan that makes sense only in the final week of college life.

The whooping and cheering was my first clue. All at once, the energy level on the streets was buzzing. I was waiting for a pick-up in front of

Sweetwater's, when the first naked man whizzed past on a bicycle. Then another. And then three naked women, a couple more men, and then a few more women. Regarding the naked men, my first thought was, "Gee, that's gotta hurt." As to the women, my reaction was, "What a terrific new way to enjoy cycling!" Meanwhile, the crowds on the street were loving it. It was like the circus had come to town.

Luckily my Sweetwater's fare was only going to the Sheraton, because I didn't want to miss any naked people on bicycles. This doesn't happen regularly. I dropped at the hotel, and shot back down the hill in time to catch a line of them turning onto Main at the corner of Mr. Mike's Pizza. There was a disciplined manner to this madness, a commando-like precision to their formation. It appeared they were executing figure-eights, swinging through the downtown streets.

Then, with a startling alacrity, the Burlington Police appeared in force. The APB must have went out: Naked People on Bikes! It seemed like half the patrol cars in the fleet were pulling up to City Hall, blue lights a-flashing. The officers sprung from their vehicles, and began methodically fanning out onto the streets. The coordination appeared practiced, as if the Chief of Police had foresaw the possibility of just such a civic disturbance, and had prepared a Naked City Swat Team, as it were, ready to spring into action at a moment's notice.

At the sign of the cops, the naked bikers split up — it was save yourself, every man and woman for him or her naked self! There was no question who were the crowd favorites in this competition. Everyone was lustily booing the blue-clads, and gleefully cheering the non-clads. Here and there, the police managed to corner and catch one, and then handcuff and haul off the naked offender to a patrol car. It looked like most of the bikers, thank goodness (if I may editorialize), were managing to elude capture and flee into the safety of the neighborhood streets.

I took up a sentry position at the corner of Church and Main — the best vantage point, I figured, to take in the finale of this evening street drama. Sure enough, I saw an officer with one last biker in tow emerge from the narrow alleyway between City Hall and the old firehouse. The poor kid at least had some pants on, but he still looked mortified. As they drew closer, I saw that he was in handcuffs. Before placing him in the cruiser, the arresting officer began reading him the riot act.

"D'ya know how stupid this is? This is disgusting." The cop was right in the kid's face. "What kind of life are you making for yourself? What the hell are you going to tell your parents when we book your ass?"

Wisely, the young man didn't say a word. From the steps of City Hall, a sergeant called out, summoning the officer.

"Don't move a friggin' muscle," he barked at the kid, "I'll be right back."

Without thinking about it too carefully — standard for me — I pulled my taxi up alongside the police car.

"Hey, buddy," I said from my window, gaining the kid's attention. "Don't be worrying about what that cop told you. You're just gonna get fined, that's all."

The guy looked at me, and shrugged his shoulders. It's hard to relax about a situation when your wrists are pinioned behind your back.

"This night," I continued, "is one for the books — one for your grandchildren. You're gonna remember the thrill of it for the rest of your life. So just be respectful to the officer, and — "

"Cabbie — you having a problem here?" The officer was back. "You're blocking traffic, so move it along — all right?"

"Hey, at least I got my clothes on!" I replied, and took off down the street.

PLEFFIC MERVYN RIG:NE

The recently completed widening of Main Street from Spear to Prospect Street is a thing of beauty, and, from the bottom of my heart, I thank everyone associated with the project. It has made a huge difference in traffic flow, particularly during rush hour.

I remember one night late last winter, when the contracting company was preparing for the onset of the construction season, and with it, the completion of the project. On the side of the road sat one of those mobile, electronic bill-board signs — the kind with the yellow letters, programmable to fit the needs of the moment. I guess the contractor had turned it on in anticipation of the imminent resumption of road work. No one, however, had bothered with the message. "Your Transportation Taxes At Work", or "Road Work Begins Next Monday" — something like that would have made sense. Instead it read: "PLEFFIC MERVYN RIG:NE". It has mystified me to this day.

I was following a Spillane's truck east up the Main Street hill. Spillane's has the contract to tow illegally parked cars for the City of Burlington, and they have the biggest, baddest fleet of tow trucks. Gleaming, steel road tigers replete with all manner of lifts, cables, and hoists, these puppies, if called upon, could probably yank a stray Russian sub out of Burlington Bay.

The Spillane's drivers are perfectly matched to the company rigs. Forget about Domino's Pizza delivery guys, wave bye-bye to the U.P.S. drivers, *auf wiedersehen* to even us over-zealous hackies — the Spillane's towing crew puts us all to shame. They fly around town scooping up the delinquent cars, maneuvering through traffic with the speed and dexterity of a Le Mans race car driver. Valuing my life, I, for one, defer to these guys.

So I trailed a safe distance behind the Spillane's truck, which was towing a sleek, little Miata on its flatbed. The Miata sported the coolest car color of the moment: forest green. We — that is, the tow truck followed 40 feet behind by yours truly — came up on the college, and then the reservoir on the right. On the left side of the road, separating the sidewalk from the street, stretched a long row of massive concrete road dividers. I was hustling out for a call at the Holiday Inn, half-listening to the Jim Bohannon talk-radio show.

Just as we passed the UVM Dairy Bar, the Miata hurtled off the rear of the tow truck, landing — whap! — on the asphalt. For a nanosecond it appeared stationary, as if oddly parked. The brain works quickly, but mine could not keep up with this mind-boggling turn of events. My first flair of a thought was inexplicably blasé: *My, this is different.*

Then the physics of the situation kicked in. The Miata took off *backwards*, as if shot from a howitzer. It careened three feet before my screeching, braking vehicle. In a parabolic arc, it spun on two wheels across Main Street, and smashed rear-end-first into the concrete barricade.

Sport cars, as we know, are magnificent pieces of machinery, fun and sexy and all that. In a collision, however, that's when you wax nostalgic for your father's Oldsmobile. The little green car, once about 10 feet bumper-to-bumper, was now about five. The rear half of the car had merged into the front half. A cocktail of automotive fluids was pooling under the front wheels. As I gazed, half-stunned, from my open driver's window, I heard the tinkle of dripping shards of glass.

About 50 feet ahead of me, the tow truck had stopped. The driver was standing in the road, both hands cupping the sides of his face, like the kid in "Home Alone".

Let it be said that this fiasco was an anomaly. Although the Spillane's guys navigate about town like there's no tomorrow, I had never before seen one of them involved in any kind of accident.

A part of me felt bad for all concerned; another part would have given anything to be the fly on the wall later that night when the Miata owner showed up — via taxi, of course — at the Spillane's service station to claim his towed car. Let's call him, "Randall" — a divorced, balding forty-something, hot and heavy into his mid-life crisis.

Having driven many such parking scofflaws over the years, I can tell you that Randall is frustrated and peeved. After a fun night on the town, the realization that his vehicle has been towed is not exactly what he had in mind for a nightcap.

He storms into the office, twenty-something girlfriend in tow, and launches into a description of his "situation".

"There were no signs at that parking lot, I tell you, absolutely no signs! What the hell is the matter with you people?!"

The beleaguered, late-shift Spillane's cashier hears this all night long, and could care less. She sifts through the stack of work orders, looking for the one pertaining to this guy's car. Then she remembers.

"Sir, did you say, "the dark green Miata?"

"Yes, why?"

"Well, there's, like, a slight problem."

"Oh, that's just great," Randall says. Maybe he turns to his girlfriend at this point and rolls his eyes. "What is it?" he continues. "Was it towed to a different lot?"

"No, it's here all right."

"Oh, 'it's here all right'," Randall says with a sarcastic grin, his exasperation rising. "Then what exactly is the problem?"

"Well, we totaled it."

It's at that precise moment I want to be that fly on the wall.

In Flagrante Delicto

The truly unexpected aspect of the fare was the destination, to wit, the New North End. Because the event itself was bound to happen; it was only a matter of time. As Jackson Browne sings, "Don't think it won't happen just because it hasn't happened yet." In my mind, the question had never been if, but rather who, where and when? The New North End surprised me for a most basic reason: from downtown it's a mere 10-minute ride. I had always imagined it would take place on a far longer run.

It was the wrap-up of a long Saturday night. The couple that hailed me were young, bleary-eyed, and attractive in a snow-boarder/hiker/mountain-biker mode. Not your junior corporate types, but not slackers either. The woman had long blond hair parted down the middle and held in place with a wide, amber headband. She was sufficiently intoxicated and/or stoned to render coming up with the house address a minor challenge, on par, let's say, with getting a correct $100 question on Single Jeopardy. I did notice her great teeth — you know, straight, white, sparkling, etc. The guy was tall and rangy. I remember he wore a new or at least very clean and pressed flannel shirt and down vest. His baseball cap had the name and logo of a rock band the name of which escapes me. All in all, a typical couple for the time and place, not unlike thousands of taxi fares I've driven through the years.

From the moment they entered the cab, closed the doors, and we drove off, she was all over him. At first, of course, I assumed it was simply kissy-face time. The taxi back seat make-out session is a time-honored courtship rite. Why wait when we can begin on-the-way? I've always believed the semi-public atmosphere — just us back here in the dark and the no-tell (ha!) driver in the front — is at least romantic, if not a downright aphrodisiac. Couples regularly smooch it up back there, and touching — of the type the nuns warn about — has been known to occur. My attitude is: have fun! What the world needs now is love, sweet love — right? As we turned onto North Champlain, however, I sensed something else underway. Or, should I say something more.

My first clue was the sounds. When couples are kissing back there, there's a sporadic undertone of whispered, cutesy repartee: "Oh, Shmookie, you are so sweet". . . "No, no, no, you're *my* Shmookie!" You know — somebody is definitely somebody's Shmookie. All such winsome wooing is delightful or nauseating depending on your individual sensibility, but in any event, it contrasts starkly with those other utterances, the sounds of couples for whom the courtship has reached its ultimate fruition — and I'm not referring to marriage.

I shot a quick glance at the rear view to observe that the female subject had mounted the male. She was straddling his thighs and hips as they kissed — and I mean *kissed*. Against all odds, the Oldie station was playing "My Baby Loves Love", as in, "She got what it takes and she knows how to use it". Over the music, the "Uhhs", "Ahhs", and "Oh yeahs" were filtering to the front. To this point, both subjects remained fully clothed.

We took the right onto the Connector — how apt that road name would turn out to be — and clothes began to be shifted from their normal — read: fully on — positions.

I guess this is as good a time as any to take a breather (Whew!) and review your cabbie's state of mind. I recall a public television documentary on chimpanzees in which the biologists created an immense, natural compound for the purpose of carefully observing the animals' social behavior. Their studies revealed that, like some woolly Mussolini, a single Alpha chimp essentially ran the entire show, including deciding which males get to mate. In his wisdom, he appointed himself sole designated copulator. I'll never forget the wistful, longing demeanor of the lesser males as they hung around disconsolately chewing banana leaves, watching their leader having sex. This sums up my outlook as the twosome in the rear began to get it on: I felt like a beta monkey.

By the time we reached the North Avenue exit, the festivities, as it were, were in full swing. How did I know? One, the rhythmic banging against the back of my seat; two, the higher octane sex grunts; three — and most conclusively — when I glanced around I found myself face to face with a comely set of bare buttocks. Prima facie evidence, I think you would agree, of the Full Monty.

For the remainder of the trip, I forced myself to keep my eyes on the road, the whole road, and nothing but the road. It wasn't easy. There's a primitive urge to watch the procreative act, and I don't think it's purely a male trait. I mean, particularly if it's occurring in the back seat and you just happen to be the driver.

Let's skip the orgasm issue.

Turning left onto their street, I heard a flurry of shuffling, zipping and giggling. If I still smoked, I would have offered them each a cigarette. The guy was smiling ear to ear as he paid the fare and exited with his partner. I watched them walk hand-in-hand to the front door.

Here's my new theme song: "Love, exciting and new. Come on board; we're expecting you. The love taxi."

Where For Art Thou, Romeo?

The cool thing was I saw it develop from the beginning. Truth be told, the entire affair was utterly and comically inane at every point along the way, an episode of spontaneous, non-stop nuttiness. It was street theater meets Mardi Gras meets Beavis and Butthead. Everyone concerned, participants and bystanders alike, kept exchanging the same dumb look which read: "I can't believe this is happening! Do you believe this is happening!?"

Okay: The corner of St. Paul and the south side of Main; the Vermont House (née the Hotel Vermont) — now converted to condo apartments; the City Hall Park and taxi stand on the north. A frisky, early autumn night, and I was idling at the taxi stand when I heard some particularly raucous disco music emanating from one of the apartments across the way. I didn't like disco the first time around, so the nineties revival gave me yet one more thing to complain about. The significant exception to my disco aversion was K.C. & The Sunshine Band, whom I loved. I saw them once on the '70's TV show, "Solid Gold". The entire band — and with the horn section, that encompassed a small squadron of members — was so obviously and thoroughly coked-out that I remember thinking, my God, they're about to either explode or implode. Nonetheless (or, who knows, perhaps because of it), they performed a kicking version of "That's The Way I Like It (Uh-huh, Uh-huh)". And that was just the tune blasting this evening from the party at the condo.

I glanced to my left and took in the venerable old building. Seven floors high, towering in its time and still one of the taller buildings in the state, its exterior was bedecked in all manner of creative flourishes — mucho, mucho rococo. One of the appealing, ornate architectural touches is the 25-foot long wrought iron balconies appended to the second and seventh floors, accessible via wide doors from the accompanying apartments. K.C., I could hear, was coming from that second-floor apartment.

Suddenly, the doors opened and a woman ambled onto the balcony, drink in hand. With the doors ajar, the music spilled out onto Main Street, and looking into the apartment you could see silhouettes of dancing figures flickering in a colored strobe light. The woman approached the railing, and for a moment stood in equipoise absorbing the street life below, Evita about to address the Argentines. Next she put the drink down, and raising one arm out to the side, began moving her hand in time to the bass beat. After a few moments of this, her hips began swaying noticeably. She was wearing a short but loose-fitting skirt, which accentuated the movement. I just happened to notice this, trained observer of phenomena that I am.

There I sat, chin in cupped hand, gazing upward, merely watching (trained observer, etc.). A guy crossing St. Paul caught sight of me in this pose, and because people are a lot like monkeys, he looked up as well. Apparently he was a heterosexual, since he immediately stopped in his tracks, dropped whatever he was doing, and plopped down on the corner bench to watch in comfort.

Another two women drifted out onto the balcony, both young and comely like the first. Maybe it was something in the night air, as soon the new recruits caught boogie fever as well. Now all three of them were laughing, dancing and generally getting down. It seemed that the public nature of the outdoor area was invigorating, let's say, to the women's spirits.

Four new guys grouped at the corner, and they were not of the complacent, bird-watcher temperament of me and the bench-warmer. No, these dudes were keen to express their delight with, and admiration for, the Vermont House party girls.

"Yo mama, yo mama! Whassup, whassup, whassup?" I could make out amidst the less articulate — thought no less expressive — background of whooping and cheering. Conscious contact was definitely established: the women were now dancing with a new vigor, all the while gesturing at the growing collection of men below.

When it comes to the hormonal response of the young male subject, a little encouragement goes a long way. Indeed, the women's response was like lighter fluid on a summer barbecue. The volume and enthusiasm of the men's mating calls rose several notches, attracting the attention of yet more rutting males who were passing by. Within minutes, at least 25 young men were congregated in front of the park, carrying on with a joyous, migrating salmon-like ardor. Lined up at the curb, a half-dozen of them took the opportunity to bend over and lower their jeans and briefs, thereby saluting the women with full buttock display, six moons of Saturn come to Burlington.

The women, in appreciation of the lovely gesture, commenced total arms-in-the-air, rotating, hip-shaking, disco-down maneuvers. Two of them wore sparkling, sequin tops, which caught the street lights in a disco-ball affect.

The escalation continued as many of the men began lifting their shirts up and down in that quaint universal symbol: Show us your breasts! Semaphore received, the women — after some evident daring back and forth among themselves — indeed lifted their tops revealing brassieres of glorious colors!

It was at this point that an older couple got in my taxi. "What the *hell* has happened to this town?" the dour man blurted out rhetorically. He leaned forward in his seat: "Driver get us home immediately; we live at Lakeview Terrace." I love when they call me "driver". Can't they see I'm a human being? If you prick me, do I not bleed?

I glanced up at a filled lavender brassiere on the second floor. I looked in the rear view mirror at the sourpusses in the back. I said, "I'm so sorry folks, but it so happens that I'm on break right now. Call Benways Taxi." This was now officially one for the books: Jernigan has turned down a paying fare.

The women next began summoning the men upstairs with circular, beckoning arm motions, like the Sirens of myth luring the Greek fishermen — into madness and grisly death, now that I think about it. A number of men dashed across Main Street, only to find the big door to the Vermont House locked. Not to be thwarted, one of them glommed onto the wall of the building, and Spiderman-style began his ascent. Here the small brick flourishes came to his aid as climbing grips. With one hand, and a mighty pull on the bottom of the railing, he reached Valhalla, as the manly throng across the street roared its approval. The women welcomed him with open arms, and they all disappeared through the doors into the party.

Two more guys were scaling the building wall when a couple of police cars arrived, and that was that. It was over as quickly as it had begun. But it had happened, it was hilarious, and now, at least, it's saved for posterity.

8

The Taxi Blues

A cabbie is often witness to the distress, even tragedy of people's lives. But unlike a doctor, lawyer or social worker, most of the time there's little a cabdriver can do to help. Finding my way to compassion, keeping my heart open in the face of such pain — this, in essence, has been my life's journey, played out in the driver's seat of a taxicab.

Refugee

A woman in her late twenties was standing at the front of the bus terminal, a suitcase in each hand. Her dress was a shift of a floral print — simple, quietly elegant. Her hair was braided, and her skin was very dark. I guessed she was from an African country.

Her demeanor evinced deep-seated worry. When fear becomes chronic it can transform a person's very being to the point that even the smallest shred of well-being and happiness desert the body. This, to me, is the genesis of true despair, the state of mind absent of hope, and the woman looked one short step from that pit. At a minimum, she looked as though she could use some help, and maybe a taxi. This was not a Holmesian deduction; people at the bus terminal are in transit — they may not need a cab, but they are going somewhere.

"Ma'am," I said, "could I help you out?" Having observed her emotional state, I spoke with as much softness as I could muster.

"Oh yes, sir," she said. "I must go to the border." She spoke with a slight French accent, but of France, not of the Quebecois variety we hear in this region.

Of course, I thought to myself — I should have guessed. Another refugee. Over the past decade, the upheavals in a number of African countries have resulted in people literally fleeing for their lives. Though we are the country with the statue on whose base it reads, "Give me your tired, your poor", our national commitment to that sentiment has waned of late. Canada, it seems, is now the more receptive harbor to these modern expatriates. Most recently, and especially since the unspeakable tragedy in Rwanda, there has been a steady stream of people from that country trying to make their way up across the border.

I said, "Okay, I can help you out. It will be $50. I can't actually take you to the customs station itself, but I can drop you at the last exit before

151

the border. From there, it's only about a couple of hundred yards to go, which you can walk."

Five years ago, before I understood the legalities of the situation, I blithely drove an entire family of asylum-seekers right up to Canadian Customs. When the agent discovered my customers were seeking refugee status, he told me that my taxi was going to be seized and I would be arrested for the transportation of illegal immigrants.

Where are the smelling salts when you need them? I began talking at breakneck speed, explaining that I'm just an innocent cabdriver, I had no idea, etc. I remember thinking if I stopped talking I was a goner. Finally, the agent told me to wait a minute, and he went back to an inner office to talk with a bunch of other guys in uniforms. After what seemed like an eternity, he returned and told me I was free to go, but my name is on record, and if I ever do this again . . . To this day, I'm convinced that he let me off the hook merely to avoid the massive paperwork my arrest would have entailed.

We drove north on the Interstate, neither of us speaking for quite a while. The big lake appeared and disappeared to our left as the wide road wended through the granite rocks and trees. In the rear view mirror, I could see my customer staring out the window into the frothy, green spring hillsides. Her mind, I could tell, was far, far away. As we passed the Grand Isle exit she spoke to me.

"There is much water in this country?"

"Well, yeah," I replied. "In this part of the country — New England — we are blessed with just about all the lakes, ponds, and rivers you could ask for."

For a minute or so she seemed to ponder my answer. "Yes, that is a blessing," she said.

"I hope you don't mind my asking," I said. "You're from Rwanda, aren't you?"

"Why yes. How did you know that?"

"I've driven a few of your countrymen over the last few years. They all seemed to have at least one relative in Canada."

"I have no relatives in Canada," she said. "I hope they will let me in. I am a teacher."

The refugees that pass through this way are invariably middle class or professionals. It takes money and education to make it this far. How could an average village dweller even know about a would-be Canadian sanctuary, let alone amass the financial wherewithal to make it here?

"Hey, it'll be fine," I said. "One Rwandan man told me there are support organizations set up to help the newly-arrived African immigrants get settled in Canada."

I was trying to reassure her, to ease her anxiety, but my words hung hollow in my mouth. How could I even imagine what this woman has been through, the experiences which drove her half-way around the world to a country where she knows not a living soul?

Genocide for her has not been a disturbing story on the fifth page of the paper, or the occasional two minutes on the nightly news. It is her life. Still, I felt compelled to say more.

"You've made it this far," I offered. "God willing, you'll find a safe new life in Canada."

"How can there be a God?" she said. "I was a Christian, a devout little girl. I had my rosary, said all the prayers." Her voice was quavering, but not close to tears. There was something in her expression that made me feel she was not capable of tears, or maybe she had long since used them up.

"What God takes away your entire family?" she asked.

That's a good question, I thought, and one to which I dared not attempt a response. Me in my blessed life, blessed country — I had no right to speak to that question.

We reached Exit 22. I dropped her off, helped her with her bags, and watched for quite a while as she walked toward the border. I watched, and I said a prayer.

A cabbie friend of mine once talked to me about the refugees. He said he always tries to talk to them with kindness and encouragement. When he drops them off, he said, he always watches them walk to the custom station, and he says a prayer. That's where I got the idea.

Mick's the Man

A working cabbie is either moving down the road or at idle, awaiting the next fare. Between the two, I prefer moving because that's when you're making money. Still, idle has its charms as well.

A few months back, as winter turned to spring, I occasionally observed a short, wiry man passing through the bus terminal parking lot as I sat waiting on the next arrival. I would observe him emerge through the wide gate in the long, tall picket fence separating Vermont Transit from the rambling, unpaved truck lot to the west. Usually with one or two dogs in tow, this scruffy guy would amble through, turning left or right as he reached Pine Street. Though clearly not in any great rush — he would side-track over to one side of the parking lot or the other as his dogs explored a promising sight or scent — he nonetheless appeared directed in his journey, not aimlessly wandering like some folks I've seen meandering around the waterfront area as the warmer weather arrives. At some point, we began to acknowledge one another with small salutary nods as I sat in the taxi or lazed in the small grassy area, though he never stopped to chat.

About a month ago, on a gloriously perfect early June afternoon, one of his dogs walked over to sniff me as I sat, Isaac Newton-like, under the sole tree, a massive cottonwood, they left standing when Vermont Transit moved here a couple years ago. After taking extensive aroma samples of my sneakers, the dog flipped over on her back and began rhythmically rubbing her body in the tall grass. Remember the toga-party dance scene in "Animal House" when the John Belushi character yells out something incomprehensible, and all the dancing party-goers instantly hit the floor and begin slithering on their backs? This was the canine version.

"Wow, man, that dog really likes you. She doesn't chill like that with just anyone."

I looked up to see the guy standing by the tree having followed his dog over to me. His fluffy, brown moustache — incongruously large on such a small, angular face — bounced up and down as he spoke.

"What kinda dog is that?" I said. "Some kinda pit bull?"

"That's no pit bull, man. She's a terrier. I got her when she was a pup about10 years ago, and she's the best dog I ever had."

The dog looked up at him from her back, scrunching up her muzzle in a doggie-style smile. "Yeah, girl. Yeah girl," the guy said as he gazed at his wriggling pooch. He spoke in that affectionate tone taken by a man talking to a beloved pet dog, a sound that falls somewhere between a father playing with his toddler and a suitor wooing his lover. "You're a sweetheart, aren't you now?"

He looked back at me and continued our conversation. "Everybody in town knows this dog. I was in Battery Park and I saw two kids playing with her. She was doing her rolling-around thing and these kids were just having a ball. A cop comes up to me and I figure he's gonna kick me out. Instead he goes, 'Hey Mick. You know who these kids are?' I go, 'I have no idea, should I?' He says, 'These are the mayor's kids. Mick, you are the man.' So then Mayor Clavelle comes over, and now he's talking to me. Like I tell you, everybody knows this dog, and everybody knows Mick."

"I see you coming through here all the time," I said. "What are you staying in the truck lot? I thought the police didn't let anyone crash back there."

"That's right," he replied. "Nobody but me is allowed to live there. I wash the trucks, and the owner of the company gave me these two old Hood milk vans. I put 'em side by side, like a two-room cabin."

The dog had arisen and was now quietly sitting beside Mick. He was patting her head intermittently as he spoke.

"That man really looks out for me. At the beginning of the winter, he asked me if it was getting cold. Next thing I know, he gives me a stove made outta a big oil barrel. He had his guys make it in the shop. I got a nice sliding door made from a refrigerator case a guy from Shaw's gave me. I'm snug as a bug back there."

"Wow," I said. "It sounds great."

I was amazed to think, in these days of strict housing codes and homeless shelters, that the city authorities would more or less look the other way and permit someone to fabricate such a substantial jerry-built home. But listening to Mick, I could see why. The guy was flat-out likable and his pet really was a sweetheart — the poster dog for "Man's Best Friend".

"What's the name of that dog of yours? She's a great animal."

Mick hesitated a moment. "I don't hardly give out her name, but like I said, she really likes you. Her name is 'Tara'".

Hearing her name, the dog glanced up at Mick, awaiting instructions. I had the distinct feeling that if he told her to swim across the lake, fetch a stick in Port Kent and swim back, the dog would do it in a heartbeat.

"What's your name, anyway?" he asked. "I see you in your taxi all the time here."

"Jernigan Pontiac," I replied.

"Jumpin' Jernigan!" he said. "Well, I got to keep moving, Jumpin' Jernigan. I'll see ya around."

I watched the two of them walk together out of the parking lot and head south on Pine.

One week later, this was the headline on page one of the local section: "Fire strikes makeshift Burlington home. One dog killed, another badly injured behind Vermont Transit." The injured dog, with "burns over 90% of her body", was identified as "Tara, an American Staffordshire terrier."

A few days later the headline read: "Burned dog dies at animal hospital. Owner accused of assaulting worker." Apparently, in his anger and grief, Mick had pulled out a knife and began yelling obscenities as he tried to remove Tara from her body bag in the hospital's freezer.

Jodi Harvey, identified as Burlington's animal control officer, said she understood Mick's pain: "She was probably the sweetest dog I've ever met — I've been crying all day." She said Tara remained good-natured until the end: "She let me pick her up even though she was badly burned and in a lot of pain. She didn't whine, growl or try to bite me." The article went on to say that Jodi has set up the "Tara Memorial Fund" to aid homeless people's pets.

So I said a prayer for Tara to help her on her way, and sent a few bucks to the Fund. And to Mick, wherever you are — you're still the man.

Hinesburg Revisited

I place my history of fares to or from Hinesburg under the rubric of "inexplicable phenomena". These runs are never uneventful; something odd or askew always seems to transpire. It's to the point that when I hear, "Hinesburg", I think, "Here we go again."

On a gloomy November afternoon, I was heading south on Route 116, *en route* to a Hinesburg pick-up off a couple of mountain roads. The woman who called needed a ride from her house to the Charlotte-Essex ferry. Right off the bat, that's peculiar. This is an expensive fare, and you can't live up a mountain without a car — so why was she calling a taxi?

I took a left at the town's lone traffic light, and drove past CVU High School. Carefully following the instructions the woman had given me, I turned off onto one of the many dirt roads and began to ascend. At 3.7 miles, sure enough there was my right-hand turn. Counting off six houses on the left — and this took another half-mile — I found the mailbox next to the red lollipop reflector and turned up the driveway.

I pulled forward to a ramshackle garage — more a shed, really — adjoined on its right to a pea-green house trailer surrounded by white plastic skirting. It appeared that a number of additions had been tacked onto the original trailer. To the left of the garage was a small, fenced enclosure. The pen, as it were, encircled an unleashed, gnarly black dog, who was doing that incongruous little grin thing, so favored by the truly vicious, man and dog alike. The dog stared at me through my windshield with hooded, rheumy, canine eyes. The eyes seemed to say, "Give me the opportunity, and I will kill you."

I waited about a minute, then lightly tapped the horn. A thirtyish woman stepped out from the mudroom into the doorway. She held a cordless phone to her right ear. She looked at me, raised the index finger of her left hand, and went back inside, leaving the door ajar.

Two minutes later, I walked up to the entrance. When I'm on the job, I'm all about let's-get-the-show-on-the-road. I gazed into the mud room and saw about six lawn-and-leaf bags bulging with clothes and household items. Also on the floor, unbagged, was a tape player and television set.

"Stanley, we've been through this. It's just not going to work. My sister in Elizabethtown is expecting me this afternoon; she's meeting me in Essex. I can't do this anymore, I just can't."

I peered through an inner door which led into a kitchen. The woman was still talking on the phone, her back to me, leaning against the kitchen table. I had walked in on one-half of an intimate, painful conversation.

"Yeah, I've heard this before, Stanley . . . No, it's not just the thing last night with my arm. What do you want from me, Stanley? What do you want?"

There was a desperate, slightly ominous sense about all of this, which only notched up my antsy feeling. I knocked on the door frame. "Excuse me," I interrupted, "but are you going to take this ride?"

She turned to face me, pressing the phone to her chest. "Load up the taxi, please," she said.

"All of this stuff?"

"Yes, all of it."

I began the loading process. I don't have a large vehicle. When I saw it on the dealer's lot, I knew it was a little undersized for taxi use, but it ran great and looked rust-free, and that's why I bought it. The woman's possessions filled both the trunk and rear seat. Loading completed, I returned to the door. She met me in the mudroom, no longer on the phone. There were tears streaking her face.

"I'm sorry," she said quietly. "Bring the stuff back in. I'm not going."

"Look," I said, "I'm gonna have to charge you $25. I'm Burlington-based you know."

"I'll pay you, don't worry. Just bring it back. Okay? Just bring it back."

"Is this guy beating you? Cause if he is, you gotta take care of yourself."

I'm not sure where this last remark came from; it just popped out. In some way, I just felt it in the air.

"No, I'm fine," she replied, but now she was not meeting my eyes. "Just bring in the stuff. I'll get you the money."

The dog watched me like a crooked cop while I unloaded. Just as I dropped the last bag, the woman came through the kitchen. Wordlessly, she handed me money, and disappeared back into the house.

Driving back down the mountain, I tried to shake the blues that had descended on my spirit. The bare trees and dismal skies weren't helping. Mine is not an abstract job, and that's probably why I like it. There's a satisfaction that occurs each time I successfully transport a customer to their destination. They hand me the money, we exchange pleasantries and the circle is completed.

There was nothing complete about this fare: I didn't get to drive the customer to the place she needed to go. Maybe that's presumptuous on my part; still it felt like the lousiest $25 I ever made.

It didn't take long. Before I had cleared the town limits on the trip back north, I had already chalked up the experience to another bizarre chapter in my history with the town. Even as I performed this mental gyration, a part of me knew I was being irrational.

The thing is, though, it did the trick. Via the magic of this make-believe pigeonhole — the "Hinesburg Syndrome" — I was able to stop thinking about the woman alone in her house, waiting for Stanley to get home. And that was something I really didn't want to think about.

8: THE TAXI BLUES

The Four Seas

A middle-aged black man hailed me from in front of the new Dunkin' Donuts on Main Street. I want to say there was an elegance to his dress, but it was more his bearing than the clothes themselves. He wore blue jeans, which appeared brand-new and were sharply creased down the front, a similarly crisp white shirt and a red, batik-print vest. He had a thick moustache, and sideburns from a mid-70's heyday. On his head was a white hat — a cap really — that I initially associated with a fast-food uniform, but then quickly recognized as the headgear worn by certain practicing Muslims.

As I pulled to the right, I couldn't get a read on this person, which is something I do automatically — student, tourist, businessperson, etc. The anomaly was the large cardboard box, slightly overflowing with clothes, which he carried under one arm. He stepped into the street, and his every movement evinced a subtle grace. When he reached my cab, he made that little corkscrew motion with his free index finger — the universal semaphore for "please open the window" — and I complied.

"Brother, could you take me to the Four Seas?" he said.

I take a quiet pride in my knowledge of all-places local, and this was a stumper. "Is that the new restaurant up in Colchester?" I asked, stabbing in the dark.

The name had a Shanty-on-the-Shore ring to it, and something's always opening around Mallet's Bay, often with a seafood theme. Thinking about it for another second — really as the words left my mouth — I realized that the name then would be the *Seven Seas*.

The man smiled. "I wish, man, I wish. No, I'm talking about the four *Cs* — the Chittenden County Correctional Center. You know where that's at, don't you, brother?"